THE ROAD TO SUCCESS

A CAREER MANUAL

How to Advance to the Top

THE ROAD TO SUCCESS

A CAREER MANUAL

How to Advance to the Top

Alexander R. Margulis

AMSTERDAM • BOSTON • HEIDELBERG • LONDON • NEW YORK • OXFORD
PARIS • SAN DIEGO • SAN FRANCISCO • SINGAPORE • SYDNEY • TOKYO
Academic Press is an imprint of Elsevier

ELSEVIER

Academic Press is an imprint of Elsevier
84 Theobald's Road, London WC1X 8RR, UK
30 Corporate Drive, Suite 400, Burlington, MA 01803, USA
525 B Street, Suite 1900, San Diego, California 92101-4495, USA

First edition 2007

Copyright © 2007, Elsevier Inc. All rights reserved

Illustrations by Tom Reese

No part of this publication may be reproduced, stored in a retrieval system or transmitted in any form or by any means electronic, mechanical, photocopying, recording or otherwise without the prior written permission of the publisher

Permissions may be sought directly from Elsevier's Science & Technology Rights Department in Oxford, UK: phone (+44) (0) 1865 843830; fax (+44) (0) 1865 853333; email: permissions@elsevier.com. Alternatively you can submit your request online by visiting the Elsevier web site at http://elsevier.com/locate/permissions, and selecting *Obtaining permission to use Elsevier material*

Notice
No responsibility is assumed by the publisher for any injury and/or damage to persons or property as a matter of products liability, negligence or otherwise, or from any use or operation of any methods, products, instructions or ideas contained in the material herein. Because of rapid advances in the medical sciences, in particular, independent verification of diagnoses and drug dosages should be made

British Library Cataloguing in Publication Data
A catalogue record for this book is available from the British Library

Library of Congress Catalog in Publication Data
A catalog record for this book is available from the Library of Congress

ISBN–13: 978-0-12-370587-7
ISBN–10: 0-12-370587-8

For information on all Academic Press publications
visit our web site at http://books.elsevier.com

Typeset in 10/13pt Adobe Garamond by
Charon Tec Ltd (A Macmillan Company), Chennai, India
www.charontec.com
Printed and bound in the USA

07 08 09 10 11   10 9 8 7 6 5 4 3 2 1

Working together to grow
libraries in developing countries

www.elsevier.com | www.bookaid.org | www.sabre.org

ELSEVIER   BOOK AID International   Sabre Foundation

Contents

Foreword ix
Preface xi

INTRODUCTION   1

DO YOU WISH TO ADVANCE TO THE TOP?   3

HOW HIGH WOULD YOU LIKE TO RISE IN YOUR OUTFIT?   9

WHAT TYPE OF CHIEF DO YOU ASPIRE TO BE?   13

ARE THERE STILL GENDER DIFFERENCES ON THE WAY UP THE CAREER LADDER?   15

DIFFERENCES BETWEEN ADVANCING IN THE TWO TYPES OF HIERARCHY: BUSINESS AND ACADEMIA   23

HOW TO BEHAVE AT COMMITTEE OR BOARD MEETINGS   31

THE IMPORTANCE OF DRESS   37

PHYSICAL APPEARANCE, GROOMING, AND FITNESS   39

YOUR OFFICE   41

E-MAIL AND TELEPHONE   45

HOW TO GAIN RESPECT AND LOYALTY WHILE YOU ADVANCE IN YOUR CAREER   49

BUDGETING YOUR TIME   53

MAKING YOUR CHIEF AN ALLY AS YOU ADVANCE   57

CONTENTS

HOW TO SUCCESSFULLY NEGOTIATE FOR A NEW JOB   67

SHOULD YOU GO BACK TO SCHOOL?   71

HOW TO CHOOSE A MENTOR AND MAKE THE BOND PRECIOUS   75

ENTERTAINING   79

FAMILY, MARRIAGE, AND CAREER   85

THE TWO-CAREER MARRIAGE   87

WORKING, ADVANCING IN A CAREER, AND ENJOYING LIFE   93

PLANNING RETIREMENT   97

Bibliography   99

Index   101

To Hedi

Foreword

I have been blessed with many favorable experiences during my career. Foremost among them was the opportunity, early in my medical training, to be a member of the Department of Radiology at the University of California San Francisco chaired by Dr Alexander Margulis. It was readily apparent to those of us working under Alex, that the prestige and excellence of the department was directly related to his unique leadership skills.

We marveled at his ability to get bright, energetic, and otherwise highly competitive people to work together, and his profound insight in making major strategic investments for the future during a time when others feared the risk of failure more than likelihood of success.

Most importantly, at the core of his persona, Alex cared more about our careers and success than he did about his own. He has served as a mentor to me for 30 years and now, in *The Road to Success* he offers the reader some of that same sage advice and counsel that have been invaluable to me in my academic career.

The late Peter Drucker was quoted on the difference between leadership and management:

> *Management is about doing things right. Leadership is about doing the right things.*

In *The Road to Success*, Dr Margulis has elucidated the characteristics of leaders that will guide them to do "the right things." True to form, rather than extol the virtues of his leadership style, Dr Margulis provides very specific advice and counsel that will be invaluable for those who aspire to rise into positions of leadership.

William R. Brody
President
John Hopkins University

Preface

My previous book, *Be in Charge*, was a success in multiple ways: Many people told me that it helped them in managing their jobs. It received excellent reviews, and was reprinted. Most of all it gave me great pleasure to write it. I also felt an obligation to share my experiences, and those of the people that kindly permitted me to interview them, with the young and inexperienced in their jobs.

The comments I heard about the book made me realize, however, that it may be more important to guide those that have not yet fulfilled their ambitions, than to preach to those that are already advanced in their careers. While lessons in leadership may benefit relatively few, helping people advance in their chosen work paths should reach many more.

It is only fair to emphasize again that my lifelong experience is in academia and as consultant to, and on the board of, several companies. I shall therefore limit my remarks to these two career paths, but as they are so broad, I believe that what follows is more widely applicable.

As it is always prudent not to depend only on one's own experience, I have attempted to review as much pertinent literature as was practicable and again interviewed many achievers in order to gain from their experience and approach. As some of the individuals interviewed have most generously revealed some intimate details about their career ascent, I have followed their wishes, and those of other interviewees, not to disclose names. I am indebted to them all. This book is an attempt to mentor those that are willing to listen and perhaps even modify their ways on how to advance in their chosen careers.

While success is in the mind of those that strive to achieve it, and many are never satisfied with the results, there are certain rules that lead to success, most of the time. I shall attempt to present them and explain why they are important. This book is once more illustrated with the beautiful cartoons by Tom Reese, by intent to bring humor to the points made in the text.

PREFACE

I am deeply grateful to William R. Brody, MD, PhD for writing the warm and flattering foreword. Dr Brody is the President of John Hopkins University, the prestigious institution that was founded as the first research university in the United States of America.

Alexander Margulis

INTRODUCTION

Integrity, self-respect and ethical behavior should be the basic rules of life on the way up.

Most young people have the ambition to advance in their chosen, or accidentally found, career, to achieve success and security for themselves and their loved ones. This partly stems from the desire to be recognized and respected and also to have parents, family, and friends feel that their faith in them is vindicated. Lack of ambition generally results in lack of achievement and low financial status, unless one inherits or marries wealth. Yet ambition must be based on some reality or it leads to unhappiness and disappointment. You need to realize that achieving success requires dedication, hard work, and sacrifices by you and also by those closest to you. Therefore it is important to ask yourself whether there is a need to go through with the relentless pursuit of advancement, or whether you will be happy to do as little or as much as is needed to be comfortable with your present situation and enjoy life.

To be successful at all costs, however, should not be the leading goal in life. Do not sacrifice the virtues that you have been brought up with. Do not scheme, lie, betray confidence, abandon friends, or plot. Even if any of it results in acceleration of career triumphs, you may regret the lack of respect resulting from your behavior. Remember that everything eventually leaks and becomes public. You also have to face yourself in the mirror every morning as you shave or apply makeup – and you want to have respect for the individual you see in the mirror.

While all of this resembles the boy or girl scout code of ethics, in the long run you will be a lot happier if you cherish your integrity, have self-respect, and do not deviate from what you yourself consider is the right way of behavior. Eventually success also depends to a certain degree on luck, on being at the right place at the right moment in time. Louis Pasteur's dictum still applies, however: 'Chance favors the prepared mind.'

DO YOU WISH TO ADVANCE TO THE TOP?

Mentoring and a sustained drive for improvement can further hone the innate gifts: intelligence, ambition, courage, physical looks, and demeanor under stress.

The advance in one's career depends on many factors, most of which are related to the individual; but many are not, and yet can significantly influence one's progress along the chosen path. To mention just a few of these: war, political turmoil, economic recession, and scandal involving the company or an important member of the university administration. Even when confronted with such external obstacles, the true qualities – talent, industry, the ability to adjust and persevere – may distinguish those that will succeed from those that find excuses for non-achievement. One's attitude, discipline, and dedication are all important. External circumstances can never be an excuse for personal failings.

To advance, an individual must have many qualities; some are intrinsic and some can be learned. Some of the intrinsic qualities are natural gifts: intelligence, ability to work efficiently, attention to detail, ambition, courage, physical looks, and demeanor under stress. Even these can be enhanced and further honed by mentoring and dedicated work toward improvement. Ambition, however, is the basic quality that propels toward advancement; it is a natural trait that generally does not require enhancement but containment, refinement, and even cruel adjustment to reality.

The basic question, however, is: Do you wish to advance in your career more rapidly then the normal path of seniority, which has institutionally determined endpoints? Or do you wish to put in the additional effort and sacrifices to advance to the top of your enterprise? The sacrifices, such as long working hours, intense reading on relevant subjects, taking courses, traveling to out of town conferences, etc., involve not only you but also affect your family or 'significant others.' Are you willing and able to learn to keep silent in meetings, until what you have to say makes an impact? Can you try to be diplomatic? Are you willing to suffer fools gladly? Can you refrain from gossiping idly? Are you strong enough to persevere in spite of downturns in your career? Are you willing to impose hardships on your family by moving repeatedly in order to advance? These are questions that test the ambition and that only a few are willing to answer with deeds.

Personal honesty, ethical behavior, respect for moral values, willingness to consider the common good ahead of your own ambition, respect for your colleagues and for the people working for you should be a given and not up for discussion. This may sound unrealistic, as cynics may believe that elbows are the most functional parts of one's anatomy, specifically designed for advancement. Yet individuals that are most successful live naturally by these ethical rules.

How does one match ambition and desire for career advancement to the top, with the cruel reality of one's relatively modest capabilities and possible limitations? The latter may be either due to one's innate qualities or to incompatibility and a poor match with the culture of the work place. One of the most painful experiences one can have in life is to have a mismatch of ambition with reality.

How do you avoid it? To be overly modest is not the solution. One of the ways is to make a list of desirable qualities leading to career success in the particular environment and another list of personal drawbacks. It can be assumed that the good qualities are positive attributes and that the personal drawbacks are negative.

What are the positive assets for promotion and professional success?

Some general attributes

> 1. Appropriate educational degrees (some university alumni groups have networks that offer powerful support).
> 2. Record of previous accomplishments (these should be carefully arranged and edited).

Some more specific attributes
In academia:

> 1. Publications in peer reviewed journals (preferably high impact journals)
> 2. Grants from prestigious organizations

3. Lecture invitations by renowned groups
4. Presentations at leading professional meetings
5. Memberships on exclusive national and if possible also international professional committees
6. Reviewer for the best professional journals (as you advance, become a member of editorial boards of these publications)
7. Successes and meritorious accomplishments of associates and students that you mentor.

In business:

1. Supervising successfully a group that before you took over, was a problem
2. Increasing productivity and reducing expenses of the unit that you lead
3. Cutting red tape and bureaucracy while increasing efficiency
4. Appointment to membership in highly ranked planning committees of your company
5. Work on national professional associations and groups in your field of business.

Other important general personal qualities

1. Diligence
2. Accuracy in work
3. Attention to detail
4. Being on time with assignments
5. Always being punctual for meetings.

Tact, discretion, good judgment, being either diplomatic or direct as required by circumstances, articulate yet not loquacious, cultured, neat, and informed etc. will further enhance your image and lead to promotions.

The negatives
*The negatives are the opposite of what was listed as positive attributes and **must** be avoided.*

Sometimes you may not be aware that you are committing errors of judgment and are creating a bad impression. How can you avoid that?

THE ROAD TO SUCCESS

A colleague with whom you work (it cannot be a competitor) can act as an umpire. Your mentor at work (it is advantageous to have one) could advise you about what mistakes you are committing. You should discuss your daily activities with your partner; he or she is an invaluable asset.

How do you gauge yourself? *You* should not. You are either going to be too lenient or too critical. A good approach is to ask a trusted, long-time friend, who is not competing with you, to dispassionately evaluate your abilities. One of the approaches that works, is to ask that friend as well as your partner to grade you separately on an agreed-upon scale containing as many different evaluation criteria as possible. Realize that the evaluation may temporarily strain your marriage or friendship, but do go ahead anyway. (Do not ask your mother to evaluate you and certainly not your mother-in-law, as you may get opposite results!)

'Number one. What assurances can you give me that you will rise to the top of your profession?'

The scale of grades for each quality is important as some of them carry more weight than others, e.g. the right academic degrees outweigh general culture (sad perhaps, but nevertheless true). Looks are very important (more in business than in academia) and can be enhanced if needed. Originality in ideas and ability to be persuasive are a *sine qua non*. Once you have been graded, and the value of grades are added up, you and your evaluator (if you are still on speaking terms) should agree on what is the expected level of qualities for the ultimate rung in the hierarchy you are striving for. If the score is marginal, you may not go as high in the present environment as your ambition aims for. The evaluator must be able to judge you by being familiar with your department or company or your university, your colleagues, competitors, superiors and the pervasive culture of the environment. Your spouse or partner, if you have been together happily for at least five years, would usually be knowledgeable enough to do that for you. In addition, as previously pointed out, you must have a trusted friend capable of mastering this task.

I am sure that we all know people that end their life deeply unhappy, because they did not reach the ultimate step in their careers that they dreamed about. However one attempts to console or reassure them, one fails. The rational way to look at such disappointments is to be grateful for the accomplishments and successes already achieved. You did not ask *why me?* when triumphant, yet you do when you fail because of what you perceive as discrimination, enmity or plain bad luck.

What are the qualities required for ascending to the top of an entity in academia or in business? It would be overly simple and inaccurate to generalize, yet some basic differences between successful people and those that fail do stand out. Academia as well as business require from a future chief: courage, good taste in choosing associates, originality, dedication to work, patience, ability to select the right plan for improving the enterprise, strength and perseverance to see it come true. The difference in requirements to achieve the top in business or academia is not major. The basic attributes needed to reach the top are almost identical.

Cynics do not believe that what they call 'boy scout' qualities are the ones that help promote people. They suspect that getting promoted requires not talent but cunning and careful complimenting and cajoling of select superiors. As an example of this cynical attitude is the following mathematical approach to what is understood to be a full effort by an employee. The formula appeared on the Internet authored by an anonymous' 'expert:' the language in the version reproduced here is slightly altered in order to make some of it less offensive.

A logical solution
Now here is a problem that finally has a formula for getting to the bottom of an age-old problem of how to get promoted. From a strictly mathematical viewpoint it goes like this:

What makes 100%? What does it mean to give MORE than 100%? Ever wonder about those people who say they are giving more than 100%? We have all been to

THE ROAD TO SUCCESS

those meetings where someone wants you to give over 100%. How about achieving 103%? What makes up 100% in life?

Here's a little mathematical formula that might help you answer these questions:

If:

A B C D E F G H I J K L M N O P Q R S T U V W X Y Z
is represented as:
1 2 3 4 5 6 7 8 9 10 11 12 13 14 15 16 17 18 19 20 21 22 23 24 25 26.

Then:
H - A - R - D - W - O - R - K
8 + 1 + 18 + 4 + 23 + 15 + 18 + 11 = 98%

K - N - O - W - L - E - D - G - E
11 + 14 + 15 + 23 + 12 + 5 + 4 + 7 + 5 = 96%

but,
A - T - T - I - T - U - D - E
1 + 20 + 20 + 9 + 20 + 21 + 4 + 5 = 100%

and
L - O - U - D - M - O - U - T - H
12 + 15 + 21 + 4 + 13 + 15 + 21 + 20 + 8 = 129%

and look how far brown nosing will take you:
B - R - O - W - N - N - O - S - I - N - G
2 + 18 + 15 + 23 + 14 + 14 + 15 + 19 + 9 + 14 + 8 = 150%

So, one can conclude with mathematical certainty that while **hard work** and **knowledge** will get you close, and **attitude** will get you there, it's being a **loudmouth** and **brown nosing** that will put you over the top.

Do not believe it! This is the talk of those that have failed.

It is important to carefully weigh the short and long term implications of career decisions. Women often feel that the sacrifices required to advance to the top are also inflicted on their family, particularly children. Seeking undesirable compromises, resulting in careers arrested at midlevel may cause regrets once the children are grown and out of the house. The 'empty nest' syndrome is a common depressing phenomenon.

Using family obligations to choose an unwanted career path is unwise, as it is generally possible to find ways to reach goals you intensely wish to reach. Compromises, delays, and help from family members and friends may make what looked impossible a reality. Perseverance and a strong desire to succeed are the key to fulfilling one's ambition.

HOW HIGH WOULD YOU LIKE TO RISE IN YOUR OUTFIT?

Every career advance requires the Faustian bargain: life becomes more stressful, sacrifices multiply.

Although most enterprises differ from each other, basic similarities between various business companies and in turn among colleges and universities remain. Whether they comprise branches, subsidiaries, affiliated companies, schools, departments, sections, etc. there are many rungs on the ladder to stay on, or climb up. Most of the time others make the decision on how high you will ascend. However, you, the incumbent, may consciously or subconsciously send signals on whether you wish to be promoted and are ready to make the required effort and sacrifices. Every step up the organizational ladder brings rewards: financial rewards with rising living standards, increases in power, self-esteem, and social acceptance. But every success requires the Faustian bargain: there is less collegiality the higher you climb, the responsibilities are much greater, sacrifices expected from you and your family increase. The likelihood of failing is proportional to the level of authority and often is related to external factors, which you cannot influence. In many instances you may not be comfortable with what the next promotion entails as it may change the essence of your activity and make you feel that you are sacrificing what you like most about your job for the parts of it that you intensely dislike. For example: in academia, a department chairman may still be able to work in the laboratory or, in a clinical department, deal with patients. In both situations the academic will be able to continue enjoying teaching. In the new position the activities least liked in the previous job may occupy most of the working time, for example full-time administration, endless meetings, fund raising, sitting at dinners next to boring people etc. In a business, promotion may result in losing contact with customers, abandoning a job where technical expertise, acquired with much effort, is no longer needed, or moving into a totally new, unknown field. And then there is the difference between line and staff jobs. To borrow the concept from the US Navy, a line job is a command position. A command, whether being captain of a PT boat, a destroyer or a nuclear powered aircraft carrier, signifies a great degree of autonomy in making decisions, provides credit for success as well as responsibility for failures. It also uniquely provides experience and pride in one's accomplishments. A staff position is one in which the individual gives advice and supplies data to the commander without making decisions. If the advice leads to a debacle, the advisor (the staff officer) usually shares the blame with the commander. If the advice leads to success, the commander is generally the only one, along with his or her superiors, that receives the credit. It is interesting that staff positions, just like command positions, can be at multiple, escalating levels, from the executive officer (a misnomer) on a small ship to the chief of staff of a fleet admiral. While in the US Navy a staff position may lead to a command, in business one may never reach an executive position from the staff post and go from lowly advising functions to high-sounding 'executive' vice presidencies. These may sometimes be very important and crucial for the survival of companies, but sometimes they are basically 'lateral arabesques' (a term from Peter's Principles, meaning a sideways move to a position without responsibilities, a face-saving job for the incumbent on the way out). If stuck in an important, high level staff position it would be a good decision either to go to a meaningful 'line' position in the same company or look for such a position elsewhere. The former may be very difficult in a centralized administration, and can be much easier if the company has autonomous businesses and/or subsidiaries.

Academia is full of advisory positions, from vice chair in a department to assistant or associate dean, associate vice chancellor or even vice president of the university. Being in such an advisory position may be very frustrating for a person used to making decisions, particularly if one sees that the recommendations are not followed and that failure is imminent. As one reaches the advisory job at a very high level after successes of command, the loss of making final decisions can be very frustrating. There are of course exceptions and they are usually limited to older individuals who have been so successful that the business or university cannot let them go into retirement before taking advantage of the last ounce of their wisdom and experience. Again self-appraisal is priceless and if you feel torn between accepting or refusing a transfer, a promotion or elevation to a staff position, get advice from trusted friends and/or family members. Always listen, keep an open mind, do not accept or refuse on the spot, sleep on it and consider alternatives. Remember however that the final decision and responsibility for living with it is yours.

HOW HIGH WOULD YOU LIKE TO RISE IN YOUR OUTFIT?

Are there special considerations that apply for women thinking about the pros and cons of a promotion? Aside from the fact that in today's society the scrutiny, at least in the beginning, of a woman executive may be more intense than if she were a man, the family hardships of moving or frequent traveling associated with a promotion, may be a heavy psychological burden. The first year in the new position is the most important period, whether in business or in academia.

You may decide against the promotion, and live happily with the decision to stay where you are: quality of life, happiness of the family, enjoying friends and the environment in which you live, may be more important than the promotion and its prerequisites. Moving to a different city is particularly traumatic for teenage children, who feel lost without the support of their friends.

WHAT TYPE OF CHIEF DO YOU ASPIRE TO BE?

One of the keys to career success is to establish a positive, unchanging image of yourself as an individual.

On the way up the career ladder you must have developed ideas on what type of chief creates loyalty and pulls a team together, as well as what are the qualities that make the opposite type of chief. The desire to become an ideal chief, when you reach that position, is only natural. The problem is that we are all different and while we may wish to be such a chief, our experiences and personality traits shape our approaches to almost all aspects of leadership. It is important to know yourself and also to have an idea of where you are headed. You must be consistent. There is no worse scenario than to be friendly and collegial with your coworkers on one occasion, and then next time around be abrasive, demeaning, and haughty. Predictability is the key to being accepted. Similarly one of the keys to success is to establish a positive, unchanging image of *you* as an individual. Again that can differ and still be highly acceptable. You may be considered a loner workaholic or an efficient, sociable, elegant, dandy, extrovert who loves people and enjoys working with everybody. As long as your image does not change unpredictably, you will be promotable and accepted by associates below you, above you and even by the colleagues competing with you. Whatever type of a rising chief you hope to become, it is essential to have plans for improvement and advancement of the enterprise that you hope to be heading. Even the best-prepared plans, however, need to be sold to decision-makers. This generally requires cooperation from coworkers and associates. If praised for the high quality of your submitted plans, give credit generously to all the people that helped you. Never gloat.

If the success exceeds your expectations it is worth remembering the ancient Roman custom at triumphal parades. There was a rider in the chariot of the man enjoying the triumph, whispering in his ear: 'Thou too art mortal.'

THE ROAD TO SUCCESS

Much of this is easier said then done. Every book on career advancement, almost every mentor, recommends modesty, kindness, and being sociable. Success, however, is inebriating; authority often corrupts. No matter how much a promising star tries to avoid the pitfalls of accomplishment, self-destructive behavior may raise obstacles to further progress. This still may not destroy one's career in either academia or business, provided that positive results compensate for misbehavior and that failing to live up to expectations is not egregious and has not become the norm. Mistakes made by popular individuals are often forgiven. When arrogant and disliked people make them, the associates and everyone else cannot wait to pounce on the miscreant. Excuses are found for those that are popular.

Having superb qualifications, being backed by powerful friends and also being at the right place at the right time helps. But like Pasteur's famous maxim states: 'Chance favors the prepared mind.' Knowing where you are headed and preparing yourself for it pays off.

ARE THERE STILL GENDER DIFFERENCES ON THE WAY UP THE CAREER LADDER?

The glass ceiling is cracking but the boys club is still in charge.

Discrimination against women in both academia and business was a fact that was not even being hidden or disguised until relatively recently. The Sex Discrimination Act became law in 1975 in the United Kingdom. In the United States Congress passed the Women in Science and Technology Equal Opportunity Act in 1979.

Legislation, however, does not change attitudes overnight. There were still well-publicized reports about gender discrimination in prominent schools such as at MIT, where a faculty committee issued a scathing report about the disparity in tenure faculty positions held by women versus men. Other schools have reacted by reviewing their faculty promotion policies and processes and found similar discrimination against women faculty members in salaries and promotions. While there are still marked inequalities, there is an ongoing effort in United States universities to right the wrongs of the past.

The remarks of Dr Summers, the President of Harvard University (until July 1, 2006), about the innate lack of ability of women to be successful in mathematics almost led to his ouster. It created a hostile group that eventually succeeded in obtaining his resignation in 2006. Yet these remarks led to debates about the differences in the development of the brain between genders. A noted woman neuro-physiologist even came up with the bon mot that 'the brain is a sex organ.' Catchy, but probably that is all it is. Functional Magnetic Resonance Imaging studies (fMRI) have shown that there are gender differences in how the brain performs cognitive tasks and how it handles emotions. Similarly, certain advanced MRI techniques (Diffusion Tensor MR Imaging) show that women's brains have more connections between the two brain hemispheres than men. There is, however, a great deal of controversy as to what all this means, and whether these findings are general and truly significant.

American society, and youth in particular, is taking this controversy in its stride. It is even becoming an object of hilarity, as shown in many funny stories on the Internet, some of which are more provocative than others. The following is a cleaner example of anonymous Internet jesting:

A Spanish teacher was explaining to her class that in Spanish, unlike in English, nouns are designated as either masculine or feminine.

'House,' for instance is feminine: 'la casa.' 'Pencil,' however, is masculine: 'el lapiz.'

A student asked: What gender is 'computer?'

Instead of giving the answer, the teacher split the class into two groups, male and female, and asked them to decide for themselves whether 'computer' should be a masculine or a feminine noun.

Each group was asked to give four reasons for its recommendations.

The men's group decided that 'computer' should definitely be of the feminine gender ('la computer'), because:

1. No one but their creator understands their internal logic.
2. The native language they use to communicate with other computers is incomprehensible to everyone else.
3. Even the smallest mistakes are stored in long-term memory for possible later retrieval.
4. As soon as you commit to one, you find yourself spending half of your paycheck on accessories for it.

The women's group, however, concluded that computers should be masculine ('el computer'), because:

1. In order to do anything with them, you have to turn them on.
2. They have a lot of data but still can't think for themselves.
3. They are supposed to help you solve problems, but half the time they *are* the problem.
4. As soon as you commit to one, you realize that if you had waited a little longer, you could have gotten a better model.

Funny, yes. But informative about attitudes!

Data from the National Science Foundation (NSF) in 2004 indicate that while three decades ago only one in every ten women enrolled in university studies earned science and engineering doctorates, today they receive one-third of these PhD degrees. *Time* magazine, in an issue in which this was the feature section (March 7, 2005), quotes the Nelson Diversity Survey that only 7% of tenured or tenure track positions in engineering and only 8% in physics are presently held by women in the top 50 US research universities. In the same survey the percentages of tenured or tenure track women in these same universities in departments of sociology, psychology and biology were 36%, 34%, and 20% respectively. One must however conclude that all these differences are most likely due to societal values and attitudes than to innate biological causes. Similarly, NSF data show that in the US government and private industry, at present, men hold most of the positions in physical sciences and engineering.

All this is predominantly cultural and is changing with time, as indicated by the fact that women, after trailing badly in numbers, have started to outnumber men in receiving Bachelor degrees in sciences and engineering (NSF, 2005). However, dramatic changes are occurring in medicine: there has been a significant increase in the number of American women publishing articles in prominent medical research journals over the last 35 years. An article published in the *New England Journal of Medicine* (July 20, 2006) based on the survey of six such journals, reports that the proportion of first authors who were women increased from 5.9% in 1970 to 29.3% in 2004. The proportion of senior women authors increased from 3.7% to 19.3% in the same period. It is of interest that the sharpest rise was in obstetrics and gynecology where the increase was from 6.7% for first authors in 1970 to 40.7% in 2004.

It is also a fact that presidents of many colleges and prestigious universities in the United States, including MIT, Brown, Princeton, Miami, and chancellors of several University of California campuses, as well as many other schools of higher learning, are now women and their appointments have generally been greeted with enthusiasm by their faculties and the public.

Every indication is that women are also increasingly encountering a level playing field in competition for promotion in businesses, but the highest positions, particularly in the largest companies, generally go to men. *The Economist*, in its July 23, 2005 issue, featured a special report on the presence of 'the glass ceiling' preventing women from rising to leading positions in major companies. In that report, however, the United States trailed only

Scandinavian countries in percentages of women executive directors in major businesses. Even so, that amounted to only 13%, while Britain, Germany and France were doing much worse, at slightly over 5%. It would be easy to assign this exclusively to discrimination and persisting cultural habits. Boys clubs and networks, and a lack of familiarity with many promising candidates by the company boards, are probably more responsible for the glass ceiling than any other cause.

The imbalance between men and women achieving partner status in major law firms is another example of the persistence of the 'glass ceiling.' According to the National Association of Law Placement in the United States, a trade group that provides career counseling to lawyers and law students, only about 17% of the partners at major law firms in the US in 2005 were women. This is only slightly more than the 13% in 1995. Yet the number of graduating students from law schools is about the same for men and women, as is the distribution of gender for beginning associates in law firms.

Promotion policies of large companies have led to class action discrimination suits, with attendant expensive judgments and settlements, but there have been some visible improvements in business promotions. Women now successfully head many prominent companies. The hiring of Katie Couric, a popular co-host of NBC's *Today* show, to become the anchor of the CBS Evening News, the post held by the venerable icon Walter Cronkhite and later by the controversial Dan Rather, is just one example of how the old barriers are falling. These advances are more likely due to societal changes in attitude and changing environments rather than to law suits.

To be realistic, it must be said that young career women do need special consideration in both academia and business. Women that are totally dedicated to career advancement and refuse commitment to marriage or raising a family are in a definite minority. Married career women that do not wish to have children for whatever reason, but more often because pregnancy and raising children may impede career advancement, are more numerous. In later years many career women regret their earlier decision and try to remedy it, either by challenging nature with various techniques administered by fertilization clinics, or by adoption. There has even been a recent trend among younger women to dedicate several years after graduation to raising a family, ignoring career or putting it on hold. What is obviously needed are programs that will facilitate the career progress of young women with children, in both business and academia.

ARE THERE STILL GENDER DIFFERENCES?

A young woman starting a career in either of the two spheres would do well to ask herself some important questions, realizing that as her life progresses, both the questions and answers may change:

> 1. Is career success your most important goal?
> 2. If you get married, would you move to be in your husband's city of employment, or would you insist that he change jobs?
> 3. Do you consider your career more important than your husband's?
> 4. Would you sacrifice rapid career rise for motherhood?
> 5. Would you consider at any stage taking a few years off from work in order to be with your child during the early years?
> 6. Would you consider returning to work right after maternity leave ceases and entrust your baby to a nanny?
> 7. What do you value more in life? To be with your family or to be engaged at work?
> 8. Do you accept without regrets that living on one family income will reduce the living standard you will have been accustomed to in a two-income mode of living?

There are no right or wrong answers to these questions, but giving thought to them may help young women in reaching decisions after considering the options and selecting those they feel are right for them.

Many career women feel guilty that they have chosen to leave their children to be reared basically by nannies. If a child does not fulfill its mother's expectations of achievement, women often blame themselves and feel that if they had spent more time at home with the child it would have undoubtedly turned out to be more of a success. There are no scientific studies that would either prove or deny this point, and so the best advice one can give is to **compromise**. Spend as much time with your family as you can, share responsibilities with your husband or partner, engage both sets of parents if possible, as they can be tremendous assets and will be able to avoid any mistakes they made in bringing you up. Instead of feeling guilty, devote as much time as you possibly can to create an atmosphere of warmth, peace, and love. Your child may still fail to become a Nobel Prize winner but you will help rear an individual that will look back on his or her childhood as a time of joy. The important lesson for a young mother is to realize that she is not alone in raising her child. Others – husband/partner, siblings and parents – should be recruited to form a compatible team providing security and encouragement.

THE ROAD TO SUCCESS

'Why, no Barbara, I don't miss being CEO of a Fortune 500 company at all.'

What advice can one give on how to succeed in her career to a promising young woman just setting out? The generalities that apply to both academia and business are equally applicable to everyone: hard work, punctuality, originality, dedication to the firm or university's goals, etc., are essential. One cannot however emphasize enough the value of good mentoring and networking with the right group. The Athena Project, started in 1999 by the British higher education funding councils, universities, and government departments, has as its goal to help women advance to top posts in science and higher education. Women business executives and women tenure professors generally love to help and nurture promising, hard-working and ambitious young women rise – until they become true competitors and rivals in their own fields. An example of the latter was the end of Carly Fiorina's reign at Hewlett Packard. A board group led by another woman (who succeeded her temporarily) made the request for her resignation.

Some older men can also be excellent mentors to young women, as often the difference in age revives paternal instincts. Such warm relationships are often examples of superb mentoring.

One particular problem faced by career women is the issue of sexual harassment and exploitation. While subtler forms will probably never totally disappear, the obvious, crude aspects of this social illness have been mostly eliminated by extremely costly court judgments and humiliating settlements. A recent judgment in California, that the boss's sweetheart is not entitled to promotions ahead of her peers, is hailed by many women as another defeat of potential sexual exploitation.

The rise of more women in business and academia to the highest positions is only a question of time. As more women reach these positions, networking will pay off. For a long time men's networking was most likely the reason that women's rise to highest positions was a rarity. The opening of leading men's colleges to women was probably the first step for networking to become gender-blind. The promotion of a woman to head a prominent entity is no longer a surprise. Neither are the female incumbent's activities closely watched, making headlines in the business section of newspapers. Being CEOs of major companies will be increasingly common for women, like presidencies of universities, or the rise of many women to leadership positions in Hollywood's movie studios. The presence of women in leadership roles is not considered to be exceptional in that milieu. (Even there networking was crucial.) We can increasingly expect that headlines announcing major appointments may not even mention the gender as a novelty, but show the incumbent's picture and provide a CV as a matter of fact. In fact that is already happening in the business section of leading American newspapers. The future is bright and is increasingly becoming the present.

DIFFERENCES BETWEEN ADVANCING IN THE TWO TYPES OF HIERARCHY: Business and Academia

In both worlds you need allies, mentors, protectors, a bit of luck, and a supporting chief.

On the face of it, the worlds of academia and business are totally different, and to be successful in one career is so very much unlike achieving promotions in the other. This is only partially true. In both one needs allies, mentors, and protectors and most of all luck.

In both so much depends on having a supporting chief and not a tyrant or personally ambitious schemer who blames his or her own mistakes on you and does not hesitate to steal credit for your achievements. While such a chief is eventually unmasked and receives his or her well-deserved demotions, in the form of a 'lateral arabesque' (a transfer to a bombastic-sounding, meaningless position) or worse, you may not have the endurance and patience to wait it out. The chances are that in your career, whether in business or academia, you will have the misfortune of encountering at least one such superior.

What do you do in order not to become another victim of such an unpleasant and undesirable chief?

1. Avoid confrontations.
2. Submit a summary of accomplished tasks in writing and keep a copy.
3. In academia, do include the chief's name on publications but insist diplomatically that he or she actually does make a contribution. This may be tricky, but as most publications in basic or applied science have

> multiple collaborators, having allies exerts pressure on those seeking a free ride. If the culture of the institution is that the chief is always included (as is the case in some European universities), no matter what he or she contributes, do not fight it; everyone knows the lay of the land.
> 4. Be patient and do your work as well as possible as no chief is above the law or so powerful that they can be destructive for too long a time. They may appear fearless, but believe, most of them are not.
> 5. Cultivate allies and friends on multiple levels.
> 6. Acquire a mentor whom you respect and who will give you the proper dispassionate and wise advice.

There are many stories of unhappy secretaries deliberately sending sensitive information 'by mistake' to someone who will harm the hated boss, or 'forgetting' to put crucial meetings with the boss's superiors on the schedule. These are just some of many ways in which tyrants pay for their misrule. And there is an abundance of people and levels of hierarchy below the tyrant who can surreptitiously make sure that the miscreant's rule is time-limited.

What can a good chief do to help you get promoted?

In academia:

> 1. Space. It is essential. A well-equipped laboratory and office, and space for your assistants, if in science, is essential. In humanities, offices for you and your assistants should be in an area that is close and has ready access to where you collect your information. Without even barely adequate space you will not be able to perform. Sometimes you may be required to share your space. Do not fight it, you may acquire valuable allies that may help you in many ways, but do not accept to make the space limitations permanent. Engage the people with whom you unwillingly share space to jointly find working space for you and them.
> 2. Funds. For some while you will have to obtain them from the department, before you are able to get them on your own. Without funding it is impossible to do the work that helps one advance in the academic pathway. Funds are also needed for your assistants. As you all advance, you as well as your assistants will be capable of applying for your own research support.
> 3. Have the chief hold scheduled meetings with you to help you progress and, if necessary, use his or her connections with other departments to find you suitable collaborators.

4. Have scheduled meetings with your chosen mentor and feel free (if this is the right mentor) to have emergency sessions if needed.

5. Your chief should show interest in your career progress by proposing you for deserved promotions. As university departments grow and need to attract teachers with many different skills and aspirations, particularly in professional schools, they have established different tracks that vary in promotion requirements. A good chief selects the appropriate track in which **you** will prosper. If you so desire and mean it, the mentor–chief will advise and facilitate the move to a track that will maximize the likelihood of your promotion and your chances to blossom and enjoy your career, rather than be continuously threatened by the ever present requirement to 'publish or perish'.

'How unlucky am I. Just as I taught my donkey to work without my feeding him, he died on me.'

In business:
A good chief does basically the same. He or she should provide:

1. Personal access and encouragement.
2. Needed space: offices, conference rooms, etc.

THE ROAD TO SUCCESS

> 3. Funds to match the requirements for accomplishing the assigned task. This will generally also mean appropriate assistants and equipment.
>
> 4. The assignment of tasks in which you excel with an opportunity to learn new ones, desirable in the business.
>
> 5. The chances to be seen and heard by other important people doing what you do best. In short: opportunities to expose your talents.
>
> 6. Support for you in your promotions. The good chief will not resist your advancement, even if that means your transfer to another department, different branch of the company or to another business enterprise.

What else does one need to do in order to advance one's career?

The obvious things are hard work, discipline, good taste in selecting assistants, modesty (but not too much), loyalty to the institution, respect for the establishment (again not blind), mastery of the chosen (or assigned) field and vision about the future, are requisites for climbing high. It is also important to be well organized and articulate, outspoken but tactful.

However, it is much easier *to fail by doing the wrong things*, which explains why so few talented people reach the top.

One of the commonest causes for failure is a loose tongue. It is easy to forget that, as you advance in your career you become more and more quotable. Praises usually do not get repeated. Slurs and juicy indiscretions do. When you are young and freely mix with your peers, many derogatory observations about other people, either in the same unit or institution, whether university department or company, are made and listened to with gusto. Some of the excited listeners will either repeat what they have heard to unfriendly ears, or worse, remember and talk about it many years later when you have all advanced and the gossip of juniors can be the cause of harm later. As gossip makes the rounds, everything gets more distorted and enjoyable to spread.

All institutions, universities as well as large businesses, generally have their own culture. A common mistake is to totally disregard the customs that everyone in the unit observes, and commit the sin of ignoring them. A foreign body is irritating. The way to avoid this trap is to try to make an effort to learn the idiosyncrasies of the environment, even if they may seem strange. Do not, however, give up your own individuality and become a cultural hypocrite.

HIERARCHY DIFFERENCES: BUSINESS AND ACADEMIA

'You have to swear Jennifer not to tell another soul.'

It is customary in smaller companies to have the CEO surround him- or herself with several levels of assistants that can deny requests or delay them by demanding more application changes and clarifications, while only the CEO can actually approve projects. Approval comes only after the barrier of assistants has been breached. This happens either through persistence or by the exceptional merits of the request. If you are one of these assistants assigned to be the Cerberus (the Greek mythological guardian of the entrance to Hades) preventing requests from going higher, do it with grace, create good will, and by all means avoid arrogant behavior. It is so easy to make enemies.

In many academic departments or businesses, junior members that are just starting are discouraged from voicing opinions about the unit's shortcomings. Do not fight the system; particularly *never* do it when you are new and do not yet know the landscape, culture, and the dynamics of the system.

There are important differences between an academic and business career besides those already discussed. The pursuit of high income is *not* one of them, as the modest, self-effacing professor oblivious of material goods and contemptuous of luxuries is disappearing. That creature is changing to one of a scientist/consultant to large companies, holder of valuable patents, usually shared with a voracious university, which is intent of renewing the patents forever, sometimes based on minuscule changes. Neither is this chase for financial 'kills' limited to scientists. Professors in law schools are also often on contract with firms or businesses that greatly increase their income, or they become attorneys in high-profile, publicity-rich trials. (Some even appear routinely on television programs.) Professors of engineering and architecture are often the highest earners on campus. Even in humanities an author of a best-seller or frequent interviewee on television can reap financial rewards. Becoming wealthy is not a handicap in academia any more. In the United States, this culture is encouraged, as a large percentage of this extra-curricular income enters the university coffers making the institutions more independent to pursue their lofty goals. Some of the faculty members' wealth may even eventually be donated back to the university to start programs dear to the alumnus.

Important differences between academia and business lie in tenure and implied tenure. Although on paper only academics that achieve a certain original productivity level, within a certain specified period, are eligible to be retained and promoted to tenure, transfer to a less demanding track or 'exceptional extensions' are common. For practical purposes and to avoid costly and sometimes embarrassing suits, being let go from a university is very, very rare. Individuals that do not live up to expectations either stay in undistinguished 'cul de sacs' or leave with great recommendations to pursue new paths, sometimes finding where their true talents lie.

The same cannot be said for a business career. There is no tenure track, real or implied, and 'golden parachutes' are a rare exception reserved for the mega-companies, and even there for very few executives, skilled in negotiation. People are let go, laid off, asked to resign or fired, sometimes at a whim, but more often for non-performance or because the company has hit upon bad times, needs to shrink, is being taken over or there is a merger, and you are one of those that becomes the victim.

How can one avoid this unpleasant but not necessarily tragic turn of events?

1. Be unique in skills that the business needs. Continue to hone them.
2. Anticipate new directions and opportunities for the business. Take university business courses that optimally lead to a degree.
3. Even in the 'best of times' work as hard as you can, and be productive.
4. Have allies and protectors for whom you are doing favors.
5. Even while you are successful and on the way up, avoid making enemies and do not slight and offend others as memories are long, especially in bad times.

HIERARCHY DIFFERENCES: BUSINESS AND ACADEMIA

> 6. Never be haughty, particularly **not** with people that work for you. There are so many ways that they can get you out of tricky traps, or watch with glee as you fall into them.
>
> 7. To quote Andy Grove, 'only the paranoid survive.'

'You are being let go Hawthorne for that time you took my parking space back in '96.'

In both academia and business there are two paths of going to the top. One is staying in the same university or company and allowing the natural or accelerated path to promotion to take its course. This is very chancy, and usually requires special circumstances. Very few people are natural 'crown princes' and being one sometimes marks you for being stopped. The other is the 'jumping from platform to platform' mode of advancement. It requires accepting offers from other universities, and in business from subsidiaries of your company or from other companies.

There are certain rules that you must follow to avoid making big mistakes:

> 1. Never move laterally, unless it is to avoid getting fired. Investigate whether the new job is really a promotion.

THE ROAD TO SUCCESS

> 2. Do not move unless you have researched through friends what the environment is in the new job and why there is a vacancy for which you are being recruited.
> 3. To get information about the company, the environment, and the job call someone who worked there and moved to be promoted elsewhere.
> 4. Do not trust any information from someone who was forced to leave or was fired.
> 5. Avoid leaving bad feelings in your present university or company. You never know whether you will not be recalled for a higher position. 'Alumni' in good standing with a fine record are generally favored for leading positions.

The 'jumping from platform to platform' approach is very hard on the incumbent's family, particularly children. If a spouse or partner has a career of his or her own, think twice before accepting to move to another city. It will cause future resentment if a spouse is forced to accept a 'step down' position or a job in an unpleasant environment. Remember that memories become rose-colored if the present is grim. The 'homes in different cities' arrangement frequently leads to divorce, as either partner may choose a new companion to listen to problems and lend support when difficulties arise.

In both academia and business you should be familiar with the benefits offered. Health insurance, disability and life insurance (their terms), interest free or low interest loans, mortgage loans, membership dues, outright contributions to individual professional accounts for travel to conferences and meetings, and of course retirement plans. Some companies and universities offer either full or a fixed amount of funds for college tuition, which in the United States, given the cost of tuition, even at state universities, may be the most enticing part of a benefit package. Do not take anything for granted, have the package explained in detail and if accepting a new position compare the packages. Take your time to study the benefits document as you may later rue the mistakes of omission.

HOW TO BEHAVE AT COMMITTEE OR BOARD MEETINGS

Prepare your material carefully. Speak only if you can improve on silence.

Committee and board meetings are getting increasingly common in business as well as in academia. They are generally held in pursuit of consensus. To reach it often takes a long time, frequently exhausting the patience of the inexperienced and those that feel that they have better things to do.

While you are advancing in rank and position in business or academia it is important to attend meetings and learn how the enterprise functions. You will also learn how meetings are best conducted, and various methods to make them more efficient and productive. Observe how certain people can obtain consensus quickly and how some need hours of discussion and have the issue eventually tabled without reaching a decision. Learning the techniques of appearing conciliatory, mild yet conducting a meeting with a foam-rubber-covered iron hand, will pay off as you advance. Pay particular attention to certain meetings:

In academia, those meetings concerned with:

1. Evolving new directions of science
2. New technologies
3. Restructuring of teams
4. Purchases of new, complicated, and expensive equipment that can be shared
5. Allocation of space.

THE ROAD TO SUCCESS

In business, those meetings concerned with:

> 1. Marketing strategy
> 2. New business models
> 3. Company restructuring
> 4. Development of new products
> 5. Company's general aims and possibly changes in direction
> 6. Opening of branches and affiliations.

In business as well as in academia, as you are promoted, you will hopefully reach a position that involves attending various standing committee meetings. Start by going to all of them. Evaluate which are important and which for you are a waste of time. Then make the decision about which you are going to skip. Do not express your future absence in these terms, but from then on send a trusted associate to the meetings you are going to absent yourself from. Your delegate should keep you informed on what is happening, as surprises may be costly. In order not to create enemies, and appear haughty, show up occasionally. You may even be surprised that meetings that you have dismissed as a waste of time are those where background preparation for important developments was made.

What makes a standing committee meeting important and a 'must' attendance? The 'usual suspects' on these committees are those where decisions on space, funds, and personnel (full-time equivalents, FTEs) are made. Of these, space is most important, as it generally gets overfilled soon after a new building or reconstruction is completed. Availability of space is also the most important factor in whether expansion of activities and hiring are possible.

Even after you have reduced the number of meetings that you go to, adjust your schedule so that you never run from meeting to meeting. Allow at least half an hour between them, as it takes time to adjust, think, and make the necessary preparations. If you are in a high enough position to have assistants, work with them to prepare yourself, reviewing the agenda and searching for hidden traps. Being prepared will generally avoid unpleasant surprises. (If you are the assistant, make sure you have researched every aspect of the project at hand and that your help is precise and valuable.)

If during a meeting you are going to make proposals that are important for your program, do not spring them on the committee or board. Think over who are the possible antagonists and present to them your proposals well before the meeting. Attempt to convince them that the proposals are not harmful to their interests and are serving the common good. Be also sure to discuss the proposal with your allies. The last thing you want to happen is to have allies turn against you.

Follow the culture of the institution. If oral presentations with handouts are the way that business is done, do not show up with a PowerPoint presentation. If a PowerPoint presentation is permissible, work on it and make it well documented, logically presented and, if this is acceptable, elegant. Do not, if at all possible, make presentations to an unfamiliar meeting, or the first time you attend a regularly scheduled gathering. Learn about the specific atmosphere, as every important meeting has its own. In basic sciences and in many schools of engineering PowerPoint is considered to be sinful; hand-written transparencies are preferred and drawing by hand in real time on whatever is available is considered virtuous.

Timing when you present the material related to your proposal is very important. At the beginning your allies may not have arrived yet. At the end they may have left. Make your act short and do not inundate the audience with unnecessary detail. Even if it is a PowerPoint presentation, have handouts ready, in color if possible. Those that need to be convinced may wish to look again at whatever was presented on the fleeting images on the screen.

What makes a good presentation?

> 1. Assess the audience, and adjust the tone and content to raise the interest, understanding, and perhaps even enjoyment.
> 2. Stay within allotted time and, if possible, make your talk even shorter. Audiences of whatever type hate long-winded presentations. (Remember few souls are saved after 40 minutes.)
> 3. Prepare your presentation carefully and rehearse timing and wording. (Reading a presentation makes you lose eye contact with the audience and diminishes impact.)
> 4. Try to be as entertaining as possible, consistent with the tastes and culture of the audience.
> 5. If you are using PowerPoint make sure in advance that the LTD and the laptop are compatible with your CD or memory stick.
> 6. Rehearse your presentation particularly if there are real time sequences or rotating and dynamic images. Audiences of peers generally do not condone technical failures during a presentation.
> 7. Your dress should be appropriate to convention and, in some events, to tradition. If you are expected to be in a tuxedo or tails (as in some European countries, particularly Sweden), or cocktail dress or

THE ROAD TO SUCCESS

> long dress for women presenters, or in a dark suit for medical or business presentations, or with an open shirt collar and sweater for basic science presentations etc., then conform! (One famous European pianist was remembered for appearing on stage for his concerts in tails and white tennis sneakers – something that audiences could not forgive or forget.) There is more on dress generally in the next chapter.

Be polite when listening to someone else's presentation. Do not whisper approval or disapproval to your neighbor and if you must ask for explanations never appear arrogant or condescending.

If the proposal presented by someone from a different department is against the interests of your unit, do not immediately attack. Listen and gauge the best time to address your opposing remarks. Perhaps some of your allies will pre-empt you, and it will not be necessary for you to come out to defeat the proposal, except in collegial support with the other opponents. If this is not the scenario and you are left alone to defend your department's, or unit's interests, ask for a delay in further discussion until the proposal can be studied in depth. This may provide the necessary time to study all the issues, and if necessary mobilize support against it.

Try to speak as little as is appropriate at meetings. People that continuously keep jumping up with questions or remarks do not generate respect. The saying: 'speak only if you can improve on silence' should be framed on the wall in every committee meeting room.

My own propensity to talk constantly at meetings was curbed by chance. During the time of my own career ascent I was a pipe-smoker, and at that time smoking at meetings was permitted. To keep a pipe lit requires continuous puffing, otherwise the pipe goes out and needs constantly to be relit. Continuously re-lighting one's pipe was even then bothersome to most people and I was therefore forced to keep puffing my pipe in silence while preparing myself to express whatever I had to say in one short sentence. This made me acquire the undeserved reputation of expressing opinions at meetings in only pithy, appropriate remarks, thus saving everybody's time and gaining undeserved respect.

If you are chairing a meeting be eminently fair – a neutral, competent, and informed referee. Do not dominate the discussion and try to keep the meeting moving along to accomplish its agenda and end on time.

HOW TO BEHAVE AT COMMITTEE OR BOARD MEETINGS

Are there any special considerations with regard to women's participation, in either business or academia, at committee or board meetings? Some particular points may be mentioned.

As we are functioning in a male-dominated society, it is common for men to express their ideas in sport-related metaphors: 'even playing field', 'dropping the ball', 'scoring the extra point' etc. Women should not be too irked by this but remember that this is still the prevailing culture. A change may be on the horizon, but it has not arrived just yet.

Women attending board meetings should be equally as pleasant as the male participants but should not allow anyone to patronize them. They should follow the same rules of behavior as those of their male counterparts who are successful, dignified, and generally well respected. In their demeanor women should never display the slightest suggestion of being coquettish or a flirt. Women on the way up should aim to convey respect, which will generate a desire among colleagues to be their allies and gallant protectors.

Dress can pose a problem for women and it is important to get it right. Dress should reflect personality but without going to extremes. Outfits should be business-like, not flashy, and adorned only by subdued and elegant jewelry. Personal wealth (be it inherited, acquired or married into) should not be flaunted.

THE IMPORTANCE OF DRESS

Your environment imposes a general dress code. Try to conform. Dress should not be a political manifesto.

There is an old belief that business executives and high position office workers go to work in smart clothes and when they reach home, dress like bums. Manual workers go to work dressed like bums and put on their best clothes after arriving home and showering. This scenario certainly holds for businesses in most of the United States. California south of San Francisco is an exception. There it is difficult from the style of dress to distinguish a manual worker from a business executive. It is only the clothes labels (Brioni, Zegna, Kitan or Ralph Lauren-Polo etc. *vs* JC Penny's) that reveal the difference. Moreover, in many companies throughout the country it is becoming a custom to dress casually (sport shirts and blue jeans or corduroys) on Fridays ('Dress-Down Friday'). These customs in effect mean that on Fridays even the CEOs of large companies in the Northeast of the United States start look like their southern Californian counterparts.

Dress in academia varies greatly according to the area of endeavor. Blue jeans, a sport shirt, and sweater is the uniform of basic scientists throughout the United States (with the sweater shed in Summer). Basic scientists seem to wish to express that they take little regard for how they dress, and yet end up in a quasi-uniform!

Academics in arts and letters are more imaginative and show more individuality in their dress. To them also, however, wearing business attire is a grave sin.

In medical schools clinical scientists and clinicians that come in contact with patients are more fastidious about how they dress. Even after they shed their white coats, a suit or sports jacket and necktie seems to be obligatory. It is this group whose casual clothes at home, on the other hand, remind one more of the manual workers at work.

These customs are easily understood. Manual workers wear the clothes that facilitate their activities, while the business people, scientists, and clinicians are observing their societal culture. Significant deviation is generally understood as protest against the accepted order or an attempt at expressing one's own individuality.

At company as well as university dinners or events there is a dress code. It is advisable to observe it. There are more effective ways to express your individuality and disagreements with policies than by the suit or dress that you are wearing. Expressing protest through dress should have been abandoned with the passing of puberty. It is ridiculous at the graduation ceremony of a Swedish university, for example, where professors and students traditionally wear tails and white tie, for a professor asked to address the assembly to appear at the podium in blue jeans and open collar shirt, without even a necktie.

The dress code at events such as family picnics, in both business and academia, is more permissive and imaginative. In the business environment it is important for one's spouse or partner also to fit into the general style.

Dress code is much more of a problem for women, except in basic science academic departments. There, blue jeans, corduroy or other similar casual slacks, with shirts and sweaters, are the most commonly accepted attire.

In business and most academic institutions career women are expected to be conservatively dressed but use their taste and imagination to express individuality. In the past 15 years it has become increasingly common for women to wear pants, in both business and in academia, particularly those women over the age of 40. In some conservative businesses, amazingly, women are not permitted to wear pantsuits. As for jewelry, the best recommendation for an aspiring career in business is that it should be tasteful, fitting but not extravagant. In academia these unwritten rules are even more stringent. Jewelry should only supplement the general appearance, never be provocative, demonstrative or dominant. Not to wear any jewelry is even promoted by many women in academia, although this has not gained widespread acceptance.

It cannot be overemphasized that it is essential to dress according to the function one is performing. When representing a company at an exhibition, for example, it is essential to wear the appropriate dress that the culture demands.

Remember that dress is only a frame; it complements the individual's substance, potential, and achievements. As a statement, however, it is more eloquent than words.

PHYSICAL APPEARANCE, GROOMING, AND FITNESS

Do the most with what you were born with. Slim, fit, well-groomed, and tastefully dressed people have advantages.

You may be very surprised how much your general appearance has to do with your career success. This is particularly true in business and academic administration. While it is politically highly incorrect even to hint that obese and sloppy people have more problems in succeeding than slim, fit, and well-groomed individuals, it is nevertheless a fact of life that the latter group enjoys tremendous advantages.

As previously discussed, dress is an expression of culture with accents of individuality. Yet casually, tastefully and elegantly dressed, slim and fit individuals are sending a powerful message. Dress, weight, and general appearance have a double effect; you feel better about yourself, more confident, and relaxed. This then radiates and is perceived, perhaps even subconsciously, by others with whom you come into contact. Moreover, if your appearance creates a generally pleasing impression people are more likely to seek and value interchange with you. There is an atmosphere of mutual respect and you may be silently admired and even envied.

Obesity is a common phenomenon in the United States and is starting to be a problem in Western Europe too. It is the result of lack of exercise and a rich, unbalanced diet. While in the past obesity was more commonly present in old age, it has in our society also started to afflict children and young individuals. Preventing obesity through exercise and a healthy diet is not difficult. Losing weight once an individual is obese is much more difficult. It takes coaching, support from family and friends and tremendous will-power. It cannot be done fast and regaining weight repeatedly is more common than staying slim and fit.

Yet being slim is almost obligatory for success in business, academic administration, the military and even in politics. This is even more important for

THE ROAD TO SUCCESS

women than men, although an obese male business mogul, university president, dean, general, admiral or successful politician is a rarity.

Certain aspects of appearance are inherited and one can do nothing about it. Height, particularly in men, has been shown to help in a career, particularly in business but also in academic administration. Many shorter individuals endeavor to compensate by becoming aggressive and exhibiting the behavior of raw ambition: the so-called 'Napoleon complex.' In reality lack of height is only a minor handicap, which can be overcome by good manners and careful grooming, with quietly elegant, coordinated attire.

Women usually do not suffer disadvantages from being short; being petite is often judged attractive. Tall women do not seem to have the advantages that height conveys to their male counterparts, but neither is height a significant handicap for very tall women.

Men are often very concerned about hair loss. While baldness cannot compete with a full head of well-groomed hair in conveying a favorable appearance, it is not a major impediment. A toupee is easily recognized and is often the subject of ridicule. (There are humorous stories of men jumping into a swimming pool and their toupee deciding to disengage and float independently!) The attempt to disguise baldness by growing the remaining hair and combing it over the bare scalp is similarly made fun of and will not command respect.

Many aging men, and particularly politicians, feel that having gray hair decreases their personal impact. Dyeing the hair surreptitiously is a common practice, but unless it is done professionally and with great care the hair can become slightly orange in color. When President Gerald Ford was debating Governor Ronald Reagan (who at that time was denying dyeing his hair) Ford made the classic remark: 'Governor Reagan of course is not dyeing his hair, he has just turned prematurely orange.'

While wearing eyeglasses (spectacles) is extremely common in academia, many business executives and politicians choose to wear contact lenses to appear younger. Corrective laser surgery is a relatively recent approach to the avoidance of glasses or contact lenses and increasing numbers of people are using this option. Many women in particular seem to prefer to avoid wearing glasses in public, but a frantic search for glasses in the purse creates an impression of a disorganized individual and should be avoided.

All the views stated in this section are general, well known and reluctantly, if not openly, accepted. While there are without doubt exceptions, they do not alter what is common.

YOUR OFFICE

An imposing office incites competition, envy, imitation, and may suggest that you are flaunting rank.

As a rising star in either academia or business you don't yet have the freedom to express to your associates, your chiefs and the rest of the world, what type of office you would like to and should have. This will come later, when you will be free to display the image you wish to project. It is a good idea to start early, showing simultaneously restraint, sophisticated taste, and imagination in using space most efficiently with all the modern technological advances for communication, obtaining information, and storage.

The office location, size, furniture, decoration, flooring, carpeting, art work, prestigious diplomas (if any), should not show self-seeking arrogance but

*'I'm just entering your office now sir.
I should be at your desk in about five minutes.'*

41

THE ROAD TO SUCCESS

should be expressing refined taste. All this will enhance your image. In essence this is similar to expressing your individuality with your clothes (discussed in the previous chapters).

Do not fight to have the office with the best view. If you win there will be resentment. If you don't, you will look inept. Choose the middle way. Your office should not be larger than the norm of offices, but if it happens that a spacious and elegant one is assigned to you, make fun of it and certainly do not brag.

There is usually a pecking order of office size and location. Conform to this, as during your career ascent the trappings of power without actually having it do not enhance your image and may even make you look ridiculous. The late Dr Julius Comroe, the legendary founder and director of the world-renowned Cardiovascular Institute at the University of California San Francisco succeeded, while in power, to curb the desire for large offices among his associates. He chose a cubicle for an office. Anyone not familiar with this symbolic gesture who came asking for more personal space left without comment after seeing the size of Dr Comroe's office. This asceticism did not last with his successors, but while Comroe ruled, it did convey a valuable lesson.

Size, location, and view from your office do not by themselves express your position in a unit. Where you stand is expressed in many other ways, and unless used as a signal, the desire for a large, plush, preferentially located office conveys insecurity.

It is important to understand that as you advance in your career you are being observed from all sides and, if successful, will be imitated. An extraordinarily imposing office incites competition, imitation, and demonstrates your possible flaunting of rank. (Perhaps still not high enough rank to get away with it.) Not doing so is particularly important when space is limited, as it tends to be in every successful operation (Parkinson's Law). If your section needs a site for small meetings (10–12 people), a conference room for your unit would be nice to have, but make sure that it is available for sharing by all colleagues or even other units that legitimately need it. Making such a facility a part of your exclusive fief creates enemies who will carry their resentment for a long time.

Make sure that up to date communication equipment is available for telephone and possibly video conferencing. Involve as many colleagues as possible in the choosing of equipment but do not allow the process to unduly delay installation. If your department or business can afford it, include

YOUR OFFICE

*'This is a video conference Adams.
I can see you.'*

---

cutting-edge technology. Remember that advances in equipment occur constantly and it is impossible and too costly to constantly keep up with them.

If you are given the luxury of choice, the furniture and the total ambience of your office, wallpaper, art work, floor, carpets, even diplomas, should be thought out carefully. It is very unlikely that you will be given the opportunity to have an interior decorator design your office. Should you be so fortunate, however, spend time to instruct her or him about your preferences and try to have the office tastefully but not luxuriously furnished. Remember that this scenario is being observed by competitors, perhaps even with envy and malice. As this may be the beginning for you of a rapid series of promotions restraint is an essential virtue.

How does one use the furniture to create the desired atmosphere in which a meeting is to take place? If you wish to discipline one of your subordinates, you must sit behind the desk with the 'culprit' sitting in a chair in front. This signals the distinction in rank. You can use this approach with your assistants, but as you do not yet have the aura of a big chief, do it only on rare occasions and only with those that forcefully challenge your status. Do not have a couch in your office until you reach a top executive position. Having a couch in the office may look presumptuous. When you have ascended in your career and your office is large enough to accommodate a couch, embrace that arrangement. A couch can offer multiple uses, including the potential for a delicious, discrete, and unadvertised nap!

If you are continuously harassed in your office by unimportant phone calls or unwanted callers, find a secluded private spot to hide – laboratory, library or wherever. This may be a place that you can catch up on your work and make detailed plans uninterrupted. Only your assistant or associate should know where you are and can beep you or call you on your cellular (mobile) phone in an **emergency**. Carry your BlackBerry or Treo with you, but turn it off. As you may still continue to engage in research or engineering work, the telephone on which you can be reached in the laboratory or workroom should remain unlisted. Time to think, catch up and remain undisturbed becomes increasingly precious as you advance in your career.

E-MAIL AND TELEPHONE

E-mail and professional telephone use have their own rules of civil conduct. Observe them.

E-mail has become the universal method of interpersonal communication. BlackBerry, Treo, personal computers and laptops have become ubiquitous, and for some people it is the routine to browse through their e-mail messages first thing on awakening in the morning and last thing before turning off the light and going to sleep at night. It is almost normal procedure to find messages in the morning from people that have sent them to you at all ungodly hours of the night. Such an important method of communication has its rules of civil conduct that one should obey.

While some feel that it is a wonderful way to answer detailed questions and messages in monosyllables or with unintelligible acronyms, it is impolite to do so and conveys the message of a lack of tact and impatience. E-mail messages are obviously a time-saving mode of communication because the date, the sender's particulars and the recipient's address are already automatically included, along with other technical identifying data. None of these details need to be looked up as they are either in the computer file or are automatically entered in the reply.

Politeness and a respect for proper form of contact should impose a civil way of expression. In Europe 'Dear' is obligatory. In the United States 'Hi' or 'Hello', followed by the first name, or only the name, is in general use to address the recipient. If you are not on a first name basis, Mr or Ms (Dr if that is the title) followed by the last name is the accepted way of starting the message. The text should be composed in erudite, grammatically correct English without abbreviations or slang. For an experienced typist the time-saving argument does not hold as the few seconds saved are at the expense of your image. This, however, does not mean that effectiveness and brevity need to be sacrificed for long-winded messages full of empty phrases.

The best messages are brief, to the point, in good English, with short sentences and proper punctuation. No message should be longer than 5–6 lines. If supporting documentation is required, this is accomplished by adding one or more attachments. Your signature should include your first and last name with middle initials only, if the person to whom it is addressed is a stranger. If the message goes to a friend or acquaintance use your first name. If it goes to someone you barely know or someone that you are not on a first name basis with, your initials will do. Your full name and e-mail address as the sender, appear on top anyhow.

Telephone communications also have their ritual. Try to dial yourself, or at least pick up the telephone as soon as the call made by your assistant goes through. Having your assistant make the connection and announce that you are making the call can be reserved for the time when you have reached the rank where this is considered to be natural, but during your ascent to that level it is considered to be showing off and presumptuous. Similarly for incoming calls, have an individual line that your assistant answers only when you are in a meeting or absent. It seems so unimportant, and is possibly time-consuming, but the impression of modesty combined with efficiency and approachability are qualities that need to be preserved. Do not have long conversations and certainly no long exchanges with your family on the 'company' phone assigned to you. When in an important telephone

'Daddy's in a third-quarter sales meeting right now Billy. I'll hear all about you going potty when I get home, okay?'

conversation, behave as if you were on television. Your voice may betray your feelings about the person on the line or your uncertainty about some of the issues discussed. All calls should be politely brief, as subsequent exchanges by e-mail may supply the information more efficiently.

Avoid making personal calls to your family during the working hours, but if you must make them, they should be brief. Avoid making private long distance calls from the office. If it cannot be avoided, make them, keep a record of them, and make sure to reimburse the company or university. Use your private cell phone for personal business. With today's digital records your calls can be easily traced. As you are on the way up, many jealous eyes will be fixed on everything you do.

HOW TO GAIN RESPECT AND LOYALTY WHILE YOU ADVANCE IN YOUR CAREER

Your performance is what really counts, but treating people that work for you, with you, and your superiors politely, loyally, and with respect is essential.

As you advance in your career, whether in academia or business, your relationship with your superiors, colleagues at similar level and with individuals that work for you, can be most helpful, or very detrimental to your career.

With superiors
Be efficient, polite and keep your distance unless encouraged to become friendlier. Even then, try not to be the one who is initiating closer relationships. This is particularly important if you and your superior are of different gender. It is easy to misinterpret the nature of a warming office relationship. Becoming involved in a personal relationship generally (with a few exceptions that end in happy marriages) may result in unwanted complications. Never initiate addressing your boss by his or her first name. He or she may start calling you by your first name, which is common, particularly if there is a significant age difference. In that case you may excuse yourself from reciprocating by citing the age difference factor and the rules learned in your upbringing. If the age difference is not a factor, use your discretion and choose the mode you are most comfortable with. Avoid being a nuisance by going to your superior's office on your own initiative or calling up with questions that you could answer by using the Internet, the department's files, or other ready sources of information.

THE ROAD TO SUCCESS

Never engage in gossip about your superiors and learn to listen rather than talk. Competitors or envious colleagues may quote you, very likely maliciously and incorrectly.

Of course, should your superior also be your mentor then much of this may not apply. You must allow him or her to set the rules of the relationship.

In the end, your performance is what really counts. *In academia*: the quality and perhaps even the quantity of your research may be more important than attractive behavioral traits. *In business*: originality of ideas, industry, meticulous attention to detail and delivering projects on time are what counts even more than being likeable. In summary, the essentials of success are: work hard, be meticulous in your performance, keep your mouth shut and make sure that what you do well is noticed.

With colleagues at your career level
These relationships are often complicated. With some you may develop a genuine friendship that is unaffected by career considerations, while with others, no matter how much you try, business and career are always at the back of the mind, theirs and sometimes also yours. It is also easy to misinterpret friendly overtures of a friend left behind in his or her career.

While you are not a chief yet, you can develop and nurture true friendships. This will not be possible later, after you have arrived: 'The captain of a ship is always alone on the bridge.' Or to quote Don Kennedy, the former president of Stanford University: 'In a dog team only the lead dog has a broad view.'

Women should be particularly aware of the fact that envy and jealousy can be potent factors in how relationships with colleagues may evolve. The difference between how women and men react to promotions of peers may have something to do with upbringing and the fact that men have been brought up in a tradition of team sports, which requires a different type of discipline, with respect for the coach, than girls are exposed to while growing up. Men also generally more easily forgive slights and insults and after even tumultuous meetings will walk together for drinks to the nearest bar. Women generally never forget insults, particularly when uttered in public.

All this loses importance if you have decided in your own mind that friendship and loyalty to your friends are more important than advancing in your career. This attitude is less common in business than in academic life.

In the latter case the solace of working long hours in the research laboratory may be so satisfying that career considerations become less important. Yet promotions may arrive almost automatically if the research results turn out to be viewed as important, and are widely appreciated and publicized. The satisfaction of activity and pursuing one's projects with enthusiasm for pure enjoyment is almost never seen in business. It somehow goes against the basic concepts of the trade.

With people working for you while advancing in your career
It is a truism that respect and loyalty from people that work for you is a tremendous asset and may significantly help your career. An assistant that organizes your workday, a laboratory assistant that makes sure that everything is properly prepared for your experiments, an aide that supplies data for your presentation, all are absolutely invaluable. Their loyalty and willingness to go beyond what effort is usually expected may propel your career and make you stand out as a hero. Yet to do this for you, these people must be repaid by equal consideration and by your loyalty to them. This is not only accomplished by politeness and thank yous, but being ready to go the extra mile to help them or their families when in need. By appreciating their efforts, mentoring them and being willing to recommend them for promotion, even if that means that they will leave your unit and go to a higher position elsewhere, you will gain their loyalty. Devotion to your staff has to be genuine; pretending shows.

The rules are fairly simple:

> 1. Do not ask your associates to do tasks that they are not equipped for.
> 2. Find the appropriate position that matches an individual's talents and strengths.
> 3. Be quick to praise and if appropriate do it in public.
> 4. Chastise in private, in your or their office. If you criticize in public, it must be premeditated as a purposeful message.
> 5. Be approachable, kind, and polite but avoid familiarity.
> 6. Do the necessary work for promotions and bonuses (if that is permitted) to recognize exceptional performance even if you are extremely busy and the effort means staying longer hours in the office. That is noticed by others and is a powerful incentive for efforts by peers to do likewise. The recipient generally appreciates your efforts.
> 7. Avoid nepotism. Never have your family members work in your section. If for some reason it is unavoidable, have them supervised

THE ROAD TO SUCCESS

by someone else and be sure to expect at least the standard quality of performance and obedience to rules.

8. Be a role model to the people that work for you. Remember that you are very visible and your behavior must be exemplary.

9. Try to create pride in belonging to your section or outfit. Remember that in warfare, which is probably the most demanding test, soldiers who are not very different from indolent individuals in other units, when part of an elite team, with a patch on their shoulder indicating that they belong, will follow the motto, e.g. 'The Screaming Eagles never surrender' or 'Who dares wins'.

BUDGETING YOUR TIME

Long hours are not a substitute for efficiency. Tasks not worth doing at all are not worth doing well.

Managing your time efficiently and saving your energy is an important aspect of life and may be the key to career success. Everyone has only 24 hours in a day. With necessary daily activities and the need to sleep for between 6 and 8 hours, obligations to family etc., what is left for work must be carefully managed. Working 10 hours, day in and day out, does not necessarily produce satisfactory results. It may tire you out and make you listless or worse, irritable and unpleasant.

The most important concept in budgeting time is to know what you want to accomplish and have an orderly game plan to achieve it. Sitting and relaxing while the clock is ticking and then having to do the job in a great rush and sleepless is a sure way of getting you to hate your job in the midst of frustration. If a task needs to be completed by a deadline allot the necessary time and make it take precedence over other activities.

Advisable rules for using your time efficiently:

> 1. Streamline the task assigned to you and obtain the best (available to you – do not be overly modest), specialized, technical assistance from competent individuals.
> 2. Have people that work for you, if you are fortunate to have them, eliminate junk e-mail and other needless communications, in order to concentrate on what is important. If you do not have access to such people try to scan your mail and do it rapidly. If you eliminate something important, do not fret. If it is crucial they will write again and mark it **important**.
> 3. Keep phone calls to a minimum and keep them as short as possible. Brevity, however, should never have tinges of arrogance and be interpreted as being impolite or uncivil.

THE ROAD TO SUCCESS

4. Do by phone calls and e-mail as much as possible and walk to other offices or laboratories only if you must. This will change when you have achieved CEO or chairman status. Then, walking around your domain will be both informative and a demonstration of being part of the group.

5. Prepare your daily schedule in advance, keep to it and if unexpected meetings or appointments come up, make sure that they are unavoidable.

6. Be on time for meetings and, if you can influence your colleagues, make them do likewise. In many American universities it is customary that meetings start 15 minutes after the scheduled starting time as everyone is generally late. Start the meeting on time even if only a few people are present. If done repeatedly it will change the habit and save an enormous amount of time if other meetings follow suit.

7. Chair the meetings in your unit, and if possible be appointed to preside over larger conferences. You will be able to start meetings on time, without unnecessary chatter. You may even be able to get them to conclude on time and with their objectives met. Be kind and civil when you chair meetings. Colleagues are easily offended and it may take a lot of time and effort to smooth feathers. Humor is appreciated only when you have reached the top position.

8. Try to avoid having meetings in your own office. Besides the appearance of trying to impress, which you should avoid, it restricts your options as it would be inappropriate to get up and leave before the attending colleagues feel that the meeting has properly ended. If you have meetings with colleagues in their offices this allows you to leave if you have to, without appearing rude, or worse self-important.

9. If meetings with colleagues or subordinates do have to be held in your office there are ways of shortening them. You can have your assistant, if you have one, call you at a specified time after the meeting has started to let you know that you are due to be somewhere else. You can then delay the end of the meeting or finish it without appearing rude.

10. If you are the one who schedules meetings, keep them to 30 minutes, if possible, and end them even sooner if the agenda is completed.

If you can, try hard to hire highly competent office staff. After a while they will learn your habits, hopefully be loyal, not gossip, and learn your taste and values. If such people are willing to follow you as you advance in your career you will have saved much effort, and each new position will start smoothly. It takes delicate judgment for your assistant to give someone an immediate appointment, or to convince others that you wish you could see them but it is just not possible at this time. Competent assistants are invaluable yet very difficult to find. Cherish and be generous with the ones that you are fortunate to have working for and with you and are willing to follow you as you move up.

Do not work yourself into ineffectiveness. Very long hours may result in a waste of time. Efficiency can save time and it can improve the quality of the product. Realize that long hours are not a substitute for functionality. Do not run from meeting to meeting. Allow time to think. Remember also that *tasks not worth doing at all are not worth doing well.*

Some people are at their best in the morning and others in the evening. Everyone on the way up in their career has to work beyond the usual 40-hour week. Try, if at all possible, to adjust the working period before or after regular hours to suit your circadian clock, as most ambitious and goal-oriented people need to work, write or prepare for future assignments beyond that usual, minimally required, time frame.

Learn to avoid looking at your watch all the time. You may be addicted to being always on time, but the clock- or watch-looking obsession annoys most people and negates the impression that you wish to convey of being sure of yourself, comfortable and relaxed.

One trick to enable yourself to still be informed of the time to the minute, is to have strategically placed clocks in your office, in order to be able to see the time without having to turn your head. (A colleague had his desk oriented to the steeple of the church across the street that was conveniently adorned with a huge clock.)

Time should be your helper and not a relentless tyrant. Do not become its slave!

MAKING YOUR CHIEF AN ALLY AS YOU ADVANCE

Your immediate superior can be a valuable ally and mentor or a threatening obstacle to your career. The quality of your work and persistently correct and appropriate behavior will propel you.

A superior – in academia, your department chairman, division or section chief, or in business the head of the company branch, company affiliate or whichever – can be a valuable ally and mentor. He or she may on the other hand be a thorn in your side, a threatening obstacle to advancement. How is it possible to make an indifferent or even an antagonistic superior into a supporter?

There are no general rules. Everything depends on you, your personality, attitude as well as your qualifications. Much also depends on the chief and of course on the environment. He or she may be a friendly individual, loyal to the staff and eager to be of help. Or your direct superior can be a misanthrope, unhappy with his or her own career and dying to take revenge on the people that have the misfortune to be part of the unit. These are extremes. Reality is somewhere in between. Generally you will neither have the good fortune to have the supportive, mentoring chief nor the ogre waiting to punish everyone that crosses his or her path. And also remember, nothing is permanent: superiors change, get recruited away, retire or even die.

Thus it is that, in whatever setting you function, almost always your old superior, the one who recruited you, or saw to it that you were promoted to the present position, has left for whatever reason. This was the superior who has delivered on his promises and kept praising you, both in public and private; a person you could rely on. A totally new individual has now replaced that ally.

THE ROAD TO SUCCESS

A NEW CHIEF

The new chief is younger, more vigorous than the old chief, someone with his or her own predilections, plans for the whole entity, including your domain and has his (or her) own ideas (including your future) that you may feel are based on prejudices. The new chief could be friendly or unfriendly to you and how you interact may make the difference between having a job that you enjoy with promises of promotions, or one that you despise. The dreaded result may even be that you may end up without a job.

*'This time he took two sips of coffee.
I wonder what that's all about?'*

Although you and your colleagues are nervous about a new chief, he or she is probably equally uneasy starting in a new position. It is the best policy to give the new head the benefit of believing that he or she is well qualified for the position and has the best intentions for advancing the enterprise as well as your career. If it happens that your concepts of what needs to be done match the ideas of the new chief, and he or she feels that you are one of the valuable assets of the entity, your life will be pleasant. You will enjoy

MAKING YOUR CHIEF AN ALLY AS YOU ADVANCE

the change and may even be on the way to a promotion. Or you may relax and enjoy your job and life, if you have given up the idea of advancing and are happy to stay in your present position until you retire. If so, you probably can from then on coast on your previous achievements.

If you are ambitious and wish to keep being promoted, you will need new ideas, fresh projects in business, while in a university your innovations and hypotheses have to result in funded grants, original publications in prestigious journals and continuing respect from peers in your discipline.

In many ways your career and the one of your new chief will be interconnected. Both of you need a new beginning, new ideas that will distinguish the new chief's tenure from that of the previous head, and you will need to work hard to fit into that fresh scenario and impress. In business you and the new chief will be expected to come up with plans that cut the budget and bring in more net profits based on imaginative plans. In a university to make your chief look successful and make him or her become your supporter, you and your young associates will be expected to write important contributions to your field. You will be expected to write successfully funded grants, win awards, prizes, medals, be members or fellows of prestigious societies and be on editorial boards of respected publications.

All of this brings pressure with it, as not only does your performance need to be outstanding, but also you are probably in competition with equally ambitious peers. How is one to deal with these pressures?

In business

> 1. Always carefully prepare your assigned material for the scheduled meetings, as requested by the new chief. Perform searches for information, read and prepare on the subjects to be discussed but do not make yourself appear eager.
> 2. Do not make your recommendations without discussions with your associates, if you are fortunate to have them, who should prepare briefs and plans based on careful review.

In academia

You will be judged by obtaining grants, publishing and being invited to lecture as well as by evaluations of your students at all levels. To succeed without having a nervous breakdown:

> 1. Realize that Rome wasn't built in a day.
> 2. Select a sub-specialized field in which you have some previous experience.

THE ROAD TO SUCCESS

> 3. Remember you must truly like and respect the field that you engage in to be able to slave in it.
> 4. Make sure that your technical help and equipment are up to the challenge.
> 5. Secure space and assistants (This is most difficult.)

The work, whether in business or academia, has to be carefully done or supervised by you, and it will involve very long days and probably also nights.

Avoid asking your new chief questions about the assigned task. Always convey the impression that you are highly competent and able to handle any task in the entity. Be careful, however, not to appear as though you are attempting to eclipse the new chief's image.

Additional hints:

> 1. Do not become a fixture in the chief's office. Proximity may be annoying and generally diminishes respect.
> 2. Continue to act within your own domain as you did before the change in the top management. You were successful before and you should keep on being so.
> 3. Never brag!
> 4. Do not give advice to the new chief, unless asked for it. Refrain from patronizing or showing that you know the lay of the land better than he or she does.
> 5. Act naturally. Do not force contact. After you have found out how the new chief wishes to operate the whole entity, cooperate and adapt without being obvious in your attempts to please.
> 6. Avoid social entanglements with the new regime beyond the sporadic contact that is customary.

A respectful distance will be beneficial to all. Your new chief should be given the privilege of working without unsolicited interruptions.

If you are asked to make a presentation, find out how your new superior likes them done. For instance does he or she want preliminary handouts, summaries or prints of the images that you will show with your computer? Overheads or only oral presentations are sometimes preferable to some, particularly to engineers and basic scientists. You may prefer flashy PowerPoint extravaganzas, but accommodate the wishes of your new chief. Always be

MAKING YOUR CHIEF AN ALLY AS YOU ADVANCE

concise yet as informative as possible. Have the slides or computer presentation in color, with graphs and figures only if this is acceptable and desired. Use as few of them as necessary to make the points. Do not give the impression of self-importance.

A hostile chief
The new scenario may be that the new chief dislikes you from the very beginning, either from hearsay or from some previous encounters that you may not even remember. He or she may have ideas about totally revamping the entity (likely without you).

'Gee sir, we seem to have gotten off on the wrong foot.'

The impression may be that you do not fit into the plans, or a new person that is to be recruited, or has even been promised your job, may be preferred. Everything about your career may be in jeopardy and promotion in the same entity totally unlikely in spite of the fact that you have been highly successful in the past. You have, however, not yet been told that you should leave.

This is the time that you have to make the decision of whether to ride it out or quit. If you decide to quit, and this may not even be a choice for you to make, you will have to decide whether to seek another position

THE ROAD TO SUCCESS

elsewhere or retire. The latter course of action is possible only if you have the financial reserves to maintain the desired living standards. If you are still young (or still feel young), that solution will be unacceptable even if you can afford early retirement. Accepting a decline in living standards that you and your family have become accustomed to should be avoided if at all possible as it is usually a quite depressing experience.

Finding another position may not be easy, as the general rule is that good jobs become available when things are going well, and everyone wishes to recruit you. Job offers have a way of disappearing when you sorely need them. Accepting a new position, without careful scrutiny, just because you are desperate for a change, may be a big mistake. Conditions may be very different from what you imagined or were promised. The move could be in effect jumping from the frying pan into the fire.

It is also possible that you have not thoroughly evaluated whether there is a chance that the situation in your present job can be turned around. Unless you have been given notice, it should be easier to find out how to get along with the new boss than to start somewhere else where you will need to learn everything about the new surroundings. If you have the impression that the new chief considers you unable or unwilling to fit into the plans for revamping the enterprise, you should examine the ideas that he or she may have presented. Try to be as unbiased as you can, and determine in your mind whether they do fit into your set of values. You may reach the decision that it may be worth while to change the new chief's mind about you and cooperate with the new scenario. This, however, should be openly discussed, and if possible, agreements should be reached on how you will fit into the new order. You may be surprised that the situation may work out; you may actually come to agree with the changes that are being instituted, which may actually have been overdue. Just because you were comfortable with the old regime does not mean that it was good for the enterprise.

If an agreement about your staying on and cooperating has been reached, do not overreact.

1. Do the best you can to further the plans that you have agreed upon.
2. Do not try to endear yourself to the new chief. Be proper, friendly and correct.
3. Avoid confrontations.
4. Prepare meticulously what you were assigned. It is courteous to send the prepared material by e-mail, fax or even by taking it to the

MAKING YOUR CHIEF AN ALLY AS YOU ADVANCE

chief's office yourself, before the presentation, to give him or her a chance to become familiar with it in advance.

5. In meetings with colleagues of equal standing to yours in the enterprise, whether in the presence of the new chief or without him or her, do not criticize or voice opposition. Never gossip. The walls have ears!

6. Realize that both you and your new superior are evaluating the new relationship and until you have both firmly decided that you are to stay, every move is carefully weighed.

7. You may, however, reach the conclusion that life is too short for you to remain in an uncomfortable or possibly even humiliating position, with a program you do not agree with or with a superior that you do not respect.

8. Liking or not liking your new chief should not enter into the equation, but for you to feel comfortable remaining in your post, mutual respect is essential.

Resign if you cannot tolerate the new situation. Do not act precipitously and attempt to get a different job lined up. 'Golden parachutes' do not exist at your present level. *Never even consider suing for discrimination or whatsoever reason a lawyer tries to suggest.* It will ruin your career even if you win or settle, which is not certain by any means. If properly handled, someone in the unit, perhaps even the new chief, may help you obtain an acceptable position elsewhere.

If you have decided to stay, the new chief has turned around and you are being included in the plans for the future, have been promised promotions and feel respected, the early negative relationship may resemble a distant nightmare, although the horror of the beginnings will probably never be completely forgotten. After a period of time, when cooperation has become almost automatic and mutual confidence has been established, the situation may become acceptable and even enjoyable.

Much of what has been said refers mostly to business. In academic life everything depends on whether you have already achieved tenure. If you have not, you are vulnerable.

Although an academic appointment with tenure is permanent, there are ways to make your life totally unbearable if your superior decides to do it cleverly, without openly breaking the university rules. Although frustrating enough to make you wish for early retirement, you may be much too

THE ROAD TO SUCCESS

young to even consider it. The same type of behavior as suggested for someone facing a similar situation in business applies here too. Be careful: do not give up and resign unless you have already been firmly offered an acceptable position at another university of similar standing and the financial burden of changing jobs will not ruin you.

Facing a hostile new chief, who is prejudiced against you, may require inventiveness, courage and coolness under fire. The following fable is entertaining, but may also provide an abstract lesson. It was obtained from the Internet, first written by a creative writer and then progressively modified by subsequent readers, including me:

The Old Poodle
A wealthy elderly lady decided to go on a photo safari in Africa, taking her faithful aged poodle named Cuddles along for the company.

One day the poodle started chasing butterflies, and before long Cuddles discovered that she was lost. Wandering about, she noticed a leopard heading rapidly in her direction with the intention of having lunch. The old poodle thinks, 'Oh, oh! I'm in deep trouble now!' Noticing some bones on the ground close by, she immediately settles down to chew on the bones with her back to the approaching cat. Just as the leopard is about to leap, the old poodle exclaims loudly: 'Boy, that was one delicious leopard! I wonder if there are any more around here?' Hearing this, the young leopard halts his attack in mid-strike, a look of terror comes over him and he slinks away into the trees. 'Whew!' says the leopard, 'That was close! That old poodle nearly had me'!

Meanwhile, a monkey who had been watching the whole scene from a nearby tree figures he can put this knowledge to good use and trade it for protection from the leopard. So off he goes, but the old poodle sees him heading after the leopard with great speed, and figures that something must be up. The monkey soon catches up with the leopard, spills the beans and strikes a deal for himself with the leopard.

The young leopard is furious at being made a fool of and says, 'Here, monkey, hop on my back and see what's going to happen to that conniving canine!'

Now, the old poodle sees the leopard coming with the monkey on his back and thinks: 'What am I going to do now?' Instead of running, the dog sits down with her back to her attackers, pretending she hasn't seen them yet, and just when they get close enough to hear, the old poodle says: 'Where's that darn monkey? I sent him off an hour ago to bring me another leopard!'

Moral: Courage, clear thinking when in danger and a little treachery will always overcome even powerful enemies!

MAKING YOUR CHIEF AN ALLY AS YOU ADVANCE

Women facing a new hostile chief are frequently confused, as it is not clear whether the negative attitude toward them is based on gender, previous record, qualifications or personal incompatibility. Before you decide which of these are valid, give it a chance and try by your competence and ability to salvage the situation and defeat prejudices. Important decisions about your future should not be made hastily and without seeking advice. You may be surprised how a period of competent performance may alter mutual expectations and clear the air. If nothing works out, use your friends to obtain an acceptable position elsewhere.

The plethora of lawyers in the United States has created an atmosphere of litigiousness. Involvement with lawyers who push for suits should generally be avoided, unless there is an overwhelming reason for legal action. You must understand that a suit will most likely freeze any future promotions, and make acceptable job offers disappear whether you win or you lose. At your present job you will be feared but marginalized.

HOW TO SUCCESSFULLY NEGOTIATE FOR A NEW JOB

No matter how attractive or unacceptable the new job offer is, do not accept or reject it on the spot. Sleep on it and in the morning your decisions will be more rational.

Applying for a new job can be a most frustrating experience. It is only slightly different whether this is a beginning position, which you are taking up right after finishing the necessary preparation in school or training, or whether it is a new position after you have already been active in a job. In the latter case, you are either dissatisfied with the position you have, for whatever reason, or you see opportunities that will speed up your ascent to higher rank. The two scenarios have similarities but also basic differences.

The first job
Applying for the first career position, whether in business or academia, has a certain ritual. The type of business, status of the university school, even the attractiveness of the job, depends greatly on your educational background. Recommendations count and so does the stature of individuals writing your recommendation letter. A phone call from a well-known person means more than most letters, as it shows that you are exceptional and worth the extra effort. If the position you are applying for has any merit you will be expected to come for an interview. You will be accommodated overnight in a hotel unless the site of interview is in the town of your residence. If you need to travel you will be given expenses. A first class ticket is most unusual, but if provided, it carries a powerful message. Interviews, whether in business or academia, follow a certain ritual, with nuances that depend on the importance of the position, the shortage of applicants or possible problems experienced by the company or academic department.

THE ROAD TO SUCCESS

A new position after you have already been actively employed
There are many possible reasons why you have left your previous job and are searching for a new position. If it has not been suggested to you that it would be a good idea to leave, and you have not been fired outright, it is most likely that you were dissatisfied with the previous position for whatever reason. Be aware that it is not easy to get a new position just because you need it. Do not apply formally for a new job. This applies for both business and academia. Make it known to your friends only that you are searching to move from your present job. True and devoted friends should then make an effort to contact their connections in companies similar to yours, or, if in academia, to their colleagues.

Being invited for an interview as an invited potential employee of the company or academic department is much more promising than applying for a job because you need it. You should still carefully investigate the new position before accepting it. In both academia and business the environment has a great deal to do with job satisfaction. A friendly boss, good camaraderie, and the possibility of promotions earned for recognized excellent performance are attractive attributes of any new job.

Investigate, personally or much better through trusted friends, before accepting the new job. If you have obtained the right information you are ahead of those that make lateral moves because they did not like their previous position and ended up with a job that was worse than the one they left.

If you are recruited because your skills are desirable, feel greatly flattered. However, it is still important to find out everything you can about the new job. Even if it is a famous university or a prestigious company, your move should not be lateral, unless this is temporary and you are being evaluated for promotion. If you can get the assurance of promotion in a letter before you start, you are ahead of the game. This is usually not done and it is generally difficult to spell out the conditions of performance unless you are in sales and figures speak for themselves. In academia it may mean obtaining research grants that partially support your salary.

After you have negotiated all the points that are essential for you to accept the new position, allow some time to elapse. The adrenaline level should be back to normal, and it is then that you (and your partner, if relevant) should evaluate the pros and cons of the new position. Try at that time, before accepting, to obtain the negotiated terms in writing. If that is not possible, or you feel intimidated by requesting it, write a letter to the individual that has to fulfill the agreed upon terms. In that letter you should state that you understand that you have both agreed on certain items (list the terms explicitly and in detail) and that should you be mistaken, you would appreciate obtaining a letter rephrasing the terms. If not, you are grateful and consider that what you have written is correct (and hence this implies binding terms).

Interviews whether in business or academia follow a certain ritual with nuances, which depend on the importance of the position, the shortage of applicants or possible problems experienced by the company or academic department.

Rules for interviews
There is a ceremonial to such occasions that seems to be general whether for a first position or for vacancy recruitment:

1. Dress conservatively. Men: dark suit, white shirt and a conservative necktie. Women: dark suit, preferably with skirt (pants are acceptable but not recommended as they may be misinterpreted as a message).

2. Get a good night's sleep before the interview and try to be calm, polite, self-assured but reserved, answering questions with short, precise replies. Avoid monologues or confessions.

3. Prepare in advance about everything connected to the position for which you are competing. The culture of the company or university department, the chief that is recruiting you, the person that you will be working for, turnovers, finances, and health of the business. Just because a company is large and powerful does not mean that it is healthy. (Remember General Motors in 2005 and 2006.) Even universities, particularly state institutions, depend on annual budgets passed by legislatures. These may have periods of financial stress. The department that is recruiting you may be somewhat immune from these difficulties, either by having abundant funds from grants, endowments or some type of lucrative practice. Assume nothing without data. Try to find out before the interview.

4. Ask questions, but do it respectfully and with tact.

5. Do not negotiate before being offered the job. It is a common mistake to believe that you have the position before it is offered. The point of interviews is for you to appear attractive to the prospective employer. Negotiations come only after the job is offered.

6. If offered the job on the spot, do not accept it right away, no matter how tempted you are. Sleep on it. Express pleasure and gratitude and ask how long an interval is acceptable for informing them of your decision. Negotiations will proceed after you have expressed willingness to accept the position.

THE ROAD TO SUCCESS

What do you wish to accomplish from negotiations?
The basics are very similar for a job in either academia or business. In order to be successful:

> 1. Find out about the true nature of the position. Its title may be irrelevant.
> 2. Inquire about space and equipment for the laboratory, offices, workroom, computers etc.
> 3. Help available: assistants, technicians, secretaries etc. (the type of help varies with the nature of the job).
> 4. Funds: in business, this will be funds to fulfill the task; in academia it will be starting research and operating funds, before it is reasonable to be partially grant supported. What proportion of your salary and operating expenses are you responsible for in the future?
> 5. Promotion opportunities: there must be a record of past promotions from the position that you are being offered.
> 6. Is the position new, and if not, why the vacancy?

Before even considering accepting, particularly if this is a relatively high position, if possible call the person that has left it and introduce yourself, or even better try to find a mutual friend who might make the call, and get all the information you can about the job. Be aware that the person that has left the job may be prejudiced.

Your conditions for accepting the position should not be immodest, as this may poison future relations. Even if the employer is in difficulties and forced to accept any conditions, do not appear to be attempting to take advantage. Be reasonable and establish friendly relations for the future, as promotions will depend on goodwill and your performance, as well as on the financial health of the employing entity. Remember that there is a long road ahead and successful negotiations are just the auspicious beginning.

SHOULD YOU GO BACK TO SCHOOL?

A second postgraduate degree can have great merits and may launch you on an accelerated track to the top.

A degree from a well-known university can be important. The college classmates and alumni/alumnae often create a club or network which opens doors and frequently is the plus that may put you on the right track. After starting the job, you are generally on your own, left to be judged on performance. The easy entry may then turn out to be a drawback as you may be watched more carefully than your less fortunate peers. The camaraderie of college days as a factor in making a career is an international phenomenon, perhaps more pronounced in the United States, United Kingdom, France, and Germany than in other countries.

Career entry trends have, however, changed in the past 20 years. A college degree was once all that was needed for a career in business; with a plethora of college graduates, a postgraduate degree is a must today. An exception until very recently was the cyber-world. Many leaders in computers are even college dropouts (Bill Gates founder of Microsoft and Steve Jobs founder of Apple and Pixar are flagrant examples), but that too is changing. Of course postgraduate degrees were always required in certain professions, such as law and medicine, but until few decades ago an MBA, an additional law degree or a doctorate were not a distinct advantage or requirement for success in the corporate business world. Postgraduate degrees were always expected in academia. But as more people get degrees, a college diploma is having almost the same lack of clout as a high school diploma of yesteryear. This is why to obtain an advantage almost everyone starting a career in corporate business needs a master in business, a doctor of law or some similar diploma. As times change, an increasing number of young or even middle-aged individuals in the corporate world and even in academia are engaged in the pursuit of additional degrees. In the corporate world it most often means a degree in law, a PhD in economics, political

THE ROAD TO SUCCESS

sciences or some other field related to the business. In medicine, ambitious academicians, if they decide on obtaining another degree, generally are obtaining a PhD. If they are interested in administration or wish to become department chairmen, deans, provosts, chancellors or even university presidents, a law degree, an additional doctorate, as for example in government, or an MBA may be helpful. Some ambitious academics in medicine may engage in pursuing a master's degree in hospital administration, hoping to use the additional degree to their MD in order to become eligible to direct a large university hospital.

'That one is the menu from the deli downstairs.'

A second postgraduate degree can have great merits and may launch you on an accelerated track to the top, but how can you achieve it without quitting what you are doing now and endangering career and family?

In a university setting, the easiest route is to plan carefully for a sabbatical leave. You may have to make detailed plans, write applications and negotiate way in advance. To be accepted into any worthwhile second postgraduate program leading to a degree, you have to be competitive and convincing. The program to which you are applying will want to be assured that you will graduate, perform the required tasks and eventually be an asset. As second postgraduate degrees are becoming more common, graduate programs, business and even law schools have started to institute imaginative approaches that are attractive for career building, for example programs leading to degrees for executives in business schools. Some of these courses are held in the evenings, several times a week, some are only on weekends and the flexibility of many is making them increasingly attractive. Many corporate firms encourage these educational pursuits by trying to adjust the ambitious scholars' schedules and even paying tuition. In some universities the tuition for faculty members pursuing an additional postgraduate degree is frequently lowered or even waived.

A significant problem complicating this pursuit is the inevitable detrimental effect on family life. Consider it carefully. Absences, additional work on weekends, and abandonment of cherished activities may have a catastrophic effect on a marriage and relations with children. This can be even more accentuated and harmful if you have to study in another town or even abroad.

How can one deal with this without destroying the base on which much of life's stability rests, the family?

> 1. Do not enroll unless you have discussed the pros and cons in detail with your spouse or partner, and the decision to proceed is made jointly. It is important that your family concur with enthusiasm. Make sure that all involved are aware of the importance as well as the drawbacks of the pursuit, and that includes you too.
> 2. As this is your additional degree, perform the needed work; try to excel but not at the expense of destroying your personal life.
> 3. Keep your partner engaged in the endeavor. Study jointly, if at all possible. Working together keeps a marriage or partnership viable.
> 4. During school intervals make up for the support you are getting by taking attractive family vacations. Be even more attentive to important dates in your family: birthdays, anniversaries, graduations, etc.
> 5. Try to obtain the additional degree you are pursuing on the fastest track available. This will shorten the time your familial relations may be at risk.

HOW TO CHOOSE A MENTOR AND MAKE THE BOND PRECIOUS

Not having a mentor can only be compared to sailing solo, without experience and without a compass.

The term 'mentor' is derived from Homer's *Odyssey*. Mentor was a wise and reliable friend of Odysseus who was given the responsibility to help and protect Odysseus's wife, Penelope, and also take care of the upbringing and education of his son, Telemachus. Athene, the Greek goddess of wisdom, the arts, industry and skill, assumed the personality of Mentor to make it possible for Telemachus to bring his father home from his long wanderings and to reassert his authority. The association of Athene with mentoring has inspired the creation of mentoring projects for women named after her, in the United Kingdom and the United States.

Everyone, admit it or not, benefits from having a mentor. It may go back to childhood, when a kind grandmother was privy to the secrets you could not reveal to your parents. She would give you sound advice and the insoluble problems would be transformed into forgettable episodes. If you were fortunate to have encountered a teacher that would spend time with you after classes and talk with you not only about the class subjects but also about the various problems of adolescence, you must have perceived the immense value of compassionate mentoring.

But you are an adult now, ambitiously engaged in a career. While the technicalities in academia differ from those in business, the substance is the same. Life is much easier if you happen to have a discrete, wise, interested and, in the best of all worlds, a powerful mentor. Not having a mentor can only be compared to sailing solo, without experience and without a compass. Mentoring is teaching and learning from other people's experience in order not to repeat the same mistakes that they have committed.

THE ROAD TO SUCCESS

There is a whole spectrum of types of mentor. They range from a severe 'Dutch uncle', to sweet talking, forgiving confidants. You may prefer one or the other mode of interaction, and it is basically not important with which approach you are comfortable, but what valuable guidance you are receiving and following.

How do you select a mentor? In many businesses and universities a mentor is assigned. This resembles a lottery. The chances of winning may be better, but the odds are that you will end up with someone who is considering it a chore, a necessary encumbrance on time that could be better spent. If this is the policy, find out from friendly old timers who you should avoid and who you should select to be your mentor. Chances are that the warm, interested, friendly, desirable mentor is oversubscribed and unavailable. Besides, they are often the very successful people who are also very busy and have a limited amount of time to devote to mentoring.

Play the game. Try out the assigned mentor. If it is a mutual waste of time, the relationship will not last and after a few encounters it will peter out. It is then that you should seek out someone on your own, someone who will not consider mentoring to be an assigned duty that must be fulfilled because the enterprise demands it.

What kind of a senior colleague would make a desirable mentor?

In academia

> 1. A full professor, highly regarded but near retirement.
> 2. An individual who has been in a high administrative position in the past, but has retired from it.
> 3. A person who has in the past been highly successful and has shared his or her success with younger associates and helped them be promoted and move on to high positions.
> 4. A retired professor who fulfills the requirements listed above, and is now only active in part-time status.
> 5. Someone who is reliving his career through your successes.

In business

Some companies will assign mentors, or have you choose from a list of volunteers who may earn points for being generous with their time and efforts. Occasionally this will work out and you may become very fond of

HOW TO CHOOSE A MENTOR AND MAKE THE BOND PRECIOUS

the mentor and grateful for the time and guidance. More often there is artificiality in the relationship, as being totally frank in answering questions may not be prudent and you, as well as the mentor may feel uneasy for perhaps stepping on forbidden ground.

Much depends on the environment. *In large companies*, if you are fortunate, the mentor may be a newly acquired friend who has been with the company for some time. That individual is doing it because he or she likes you, and thus mentoring becomes what it can be at its best: spontaneous, unassigned, informal, discrete. A timing clock is never involved. Such friend–mentors are often doing this because it helps them escape the anonymity of a large company, and by adopting you, they enjoy pointing out the traps and hidden minefields that perhaps they have not been able to avoid. The only benefits that these spontaneous well-meaning amateur mentors derive from this exercise are the pleasure of seeing you succeed and the feeling that they have played a meaningful role in it. Meetings are not scheduled according to an established plan, and there is no ritual or note taking. You meet whenever there is a necessity for it, so perceived by you or when the mentor is informed about policy changes that may affect you. Such a mentor should be cherished as they are not the norm and you may have to invest time and much effort to find such a paragon.

In a small company finding the right sponsor may be much more difficult. Often it is the person in a high position in the company that has recommended your hiring and may feel responsible for your performance. In a small company such a person is generally very busy and the informal sessions may occur only if you request them, or more likely, if someone higher up feels that you show great promise and wishes to help you for the good of the company. One wishes that the reverse is not the reason for the need for mentoring: hopefully it is not remedial.

The CEO of the small company is most often so busy keeping it afloat that he or she cannot spare the time to enjoy mentoring a promising greenhorn like you.

A note of caution for young women: In none of the scenarios discussed, whether a university, large or small company, should sexual overtones, open or hidden, ever be permitted. As mentoring is an exercise in which often very intimate issues are discussed, the mentor and you are bonding. Unless the relationship is kept at a level of filial or fraternal intimacy, severe complications may be the unwanted side effects, with the potential to destroy

THE ROAD TO SUCCESS

the careers of both participants. This is easier said than done. Bonding may remain at a high level if both participants are of the same gender or the mentor is very much older than the mentee.

A different type of mentoring, often much more effective, yet sometimes resented, occurs when family members attempt to guide you. Generally such advice is graciously accepted only from grandparents or perhaps from older brothers or sisters. Parents and spouses could be very helpful, but their advice is generally followed only in major crises.

ENTERTAINING

The basic rule of entertainment is to be warm, friendly, and hospitable. Avoid appearing snobbish, miserly or extravagant.

Entertaining means sharing one's privacy, time and hospitality with other people. There is a great difference between private and business-related entertaining. As you ascend in your career the latter becomes more frequent, and doing it well assumes increasing importance. Depending on whom you are entertaining, people that work for you, equals, superiors or other important guests, the rules change. They are different also where you are entertaining your guests in a restaurant or at home, with or without partners.

The basic maxim about entertainment is not to appear snobbish, miserly or extravagant. Try to convey your own personal touch and taste, regardless of the occasion. Entertain without trying to impress. Do it the way you feel most comfortable, using your own values. Try to be hospitable and accommodate the religious restrictions of your guests. Observant Roman Catholics, orthodox Jews, pious Moslems and so many other groups in our heterogeneous society have their dietary rules and taboos. You should be cognizant of them and avoid committing a *faux pas*, when all you really want is to be kind and hospitable.

Entertaining superiors at a restaurant
First of all find out the taste of your guest, but also make sure, should it be very different from yours, that you find a compromise. There is no need to be uncomfortable with a restaurant or food that you despise, and certainly it is not proper to be lavish or extravagant. If you take your chief or another superior to a modest neighborhood restaurant do it because you have been there before and it is special. Do not try to impress the superior about your frugality as it may be interpreted that you are using the occasion to show that you need a raise in salary. Your choice of restaurant signals respect and thoughtfulness in selecting the ambience and cuisine that will please the individual. It also reflects your own taste. The latter is

important. You do not wish to appear lacking in taste. If you have a restaurant where you will be recognized, remembered, greeted by name and seated quickly you will earn points. Waiting in a corridor or being sent to the bar where some of you may not even get a seat is unimpressive, can be embarrassing and is certainly annoying, although your guests will probably not blame you for it.

Do not reserve a private room for your dinner, unless there is a special celebration. A private room may be a necessity if there is a large group, you are not the only host, there is a special occasion to be celebrated, and privacy is required. If the group is small, cocktails should be drunk at the table. If the group numbers more than eight you may ask for another room where cocktails may be enjoyed, but for not more than half an hour. The cost of the drinks should be included in the dinner bill. Anything else, like a cash bar, would be a catastrophe.

It cannot be over-emphasized that you must be careful about how much you drink. Some governments test potential recruits for the foreign or intelligence services with dinners at which very fine quality wines and liquor are served. Any recruit who is unable to control his or her drinking is obviously a security risk. At the dinner that you host by yourself or with colleagues, you should try to stay with wine and drink not more than two glasses during the whole evening. If your guest is a tee-totaler you should abstain too, out of respect, but do not make a show of it.

If the party is smaller than eight (which will generally be the case, unless it is a special occasion), then everyone should order 'à la carte'. For larger parties, that you have been assigned to arrange for the group, it is advantageous to provide three fixed menu choices: a meat dish (lamb or veal is usually preferred by most guests; avoid beef and pork), fish and a vegetarian option. Your guests could be offered the chance to make their selection when accepting the invitation but it could also be done at the dinner table, particularly if the group is not very large. Selecting the main dish in advance saves time and considerably simplifies ordering for large dinner parties.

With one's chief, whether in business or university, the dinner is rarely a purely social event. If the dinner is with partners and is a quasi-social occasion, try to have the conversation flowing, particularly in the area of the guest's interest. This will require some discrete preliminary research. Try not to discuss politics, religion, the endangered environment or similar subjects that may provoke confrontations. It is easy, particularly with some guests holding passionate views, to spoil an otherwise carefully planned occasion.

ENTERTAINING

Seating is very important if the party is larger than eight. Everyone in the room wants to sit next to the chief or guest of honor. Those who sit near the periphery will feel slighted and resentful, and they may think that you have made these arrangements on purpose. To try to avoid ruffled feathers, seat the guest of honor centrally and mix guests as much as possible. If the meal includes partners too, try to seat guests with shared interests next to each other. The worst mistake you can make is to have the guest of honor and everyone 'important' sit at one end of the table and all others of lower rank sit at the other end. They will consider they have been relegated to 'Siberia'. Realize that usually not more than four people, and at maximum six, can actively participate in a conversation. Avoid and discourage (unless it is the guest of honor), a loud 'lecture' to the group. Do not yourself praise the restaurant or the food. If you did not like it, you would not have selected it. Praising reveals insecurity and a desire to be reassured.

Dress for the evening depends greatly on whether the dinner is right after work or there is an intervening period of at least one hour. A suit or blazer, even a sports jacket and pants, are now acceptable. Clean shirt and necktie are a must. For women a suit, with skirt or pants, or a dress is fine. Use jewelry that supports the accent of the dress. Overly casual clothing for both men and women (such as blue jeans and a sweater) is almost a political statement and should be avoided.

Entertaining superiors at your own home
Having your chief for dinner at your home requires careful orchestration, yet it must appear spontaneous and natural. Unless you and your partner, and your superior and his or her partner, are celebrating a special, perhaps joint occasion, invite one and not more than two other couples that have interests and backgrounds that would make the evening enjoyable and interesting. If you can afford it, have the event catered. It is a good investment as neither you nor your spouse should run around serving, refilling glasses or removing dishes. If you have help, or if you or your partner are serving the food and drinks, it should be done quietly and unobtrusively.

The meal requires careful planning. Try to find out what the main guest and other guests like. Exclude what they do not eat for whatever reason. Wines should be appropriate and not ostentatiously expensive. Port, Armagnac, Cognac or liqueurs after dinner add a special touch. In Cognacs try to offer X-O quality; Armagnac should have a vintage. Cigars used to be a special attraction after a good dinner – no more!

The dinner conversation should not be only about the office or laboratory, as probably half of the guests will not be interested in that subject. Be aware

THE ROAD TO SUCCESS

of the conversation that is going on. Political, religious or other potentially divisive subjects can cause clashes that can ruin your carefully arranged party. Sometimes you need to steer the conversation away from sensitive subjects.

Lunches with superiors
Lunches are much simpler but still require planning. Remember that the old 'two Martini lunch' is distant history. The kind of lunch that you might be hosting is usually held in a neighboring restaurant or in a club. In a university it would be the faculty club, of which you ought to be a member. The lunch menu should be simple, but if possible have at least two choices. It is advisable to find out what your superior likes for lunch and choose a restaurant serving an appropriate menu. Having lunch at a restaurant close to the place of work shows that you value time, as you are not taking your guest to a famous eating place some distance away. It is not advisable to include many people at such lunches. In a small group everyone can order what she or he likes. As one is generally expected to return to work in the afternoon, do not order a bottle of wine and certainly Martinis or similar hard liquor are out.

A lunch with your superior inevitably involves some business conversation. It is important, therefore, to have tables out of earshot of others. If this is not possible, no business talk should be conducted at the table. One never

'In my day we would have been on our third martini by now.'

ENTERTAINING

knows who is listening. In the conversation have an optimistic, pleasant order of subjects. If there are painful topics that have to be dealt with, they should not be discussed at or even after lunch. If possible, select another occasion. Such business would only spoil the meal.

Entertaining equals
There is not much to be added to what was said above, except that entertaining equals almost never involves business. If it is business, then it is not entertaining and can be performed efficiently at lunch, or in each other's office. If there is an agenda, and it is longer than can be handled during a lunch, and if it needs to be connected to a dinner, have it in a restaurant not too far from the office. No alcoholic beverages should be served at business lunches, and also limit alcohol consumption at business dinners.

When it comes to entertaining equals, there should be a difference in ambience if the evening dinner, or weekend lunch, is a celebration of some kind, or if it is a just a pleasant occasion to be together. Often it is a repayment for having been entertained previously. Among equals there should not be any rules other than that a social get-together should be an enjoyable occasion that will bring the participants closer. Always remember that equals can be important allies, and that fostering friendships through entertaining should be natural and pleasant, whether at home, in a restaurant, country outing or away from the city where you live.

If you go out together often, share the bill. It avoids wrestling for the check and it eliminates feeling obligated and remembering who paid the last time out.

Entertaining individuals that work for you
Whether in business or in a university, as your career advances you will have assistants, secretaries or laboratory technicians. Although you are not their employer, but the company or the university is, they do work with you and take directions from you. It is essential that a friendly bond be developed based on mutual respect and after a while, mutual loyalty.

While gifts at Christmas are obligatory, and by now have become cultural traditions, little gifts for special occasions – birthdays, promotions, engagement etc. – are always appreciated. If you are returning from an interesting journey, particularly from an intriguing or quaint part of the world, bringing a gift unique to that country, shows that your assistant was in your thoughts.

Try to take your assistant, technician or helper for lunch at least once or twice a year. It does not have to be a special occasion. If it is spontaneous

THE ROAD TO SUCCESS

it is a signal that you are truly appreciative of their efforts. Neighborhood restaurants or the faculty club in a university should be the locale. Never take them to the cafeteria where they may have their usual meals. It would be interpreted that you are a miser and lack both taste and appreciation.

If there is gender difference, have at least two guests in order to avoid any misinterpretation.

If you are invited to a celebration by one of your assistants make every effort to attend and bring or send an appropriate gift. Sadly this also applies to memorials or funerals, of the assistants themselves or members of their family. For such an event, send a wreath or flowers and a warm letter of condolence.

FAMILY, MARRIAGE, AND CAREER

Family and marriage should come first whenever there is a conflict with the job.

As you climb in your career, work long hours, travel to meetings or conventions, it is easy to forget that it is your partner, your family, who provide the safe harbor to which you return, the base on which everything else rests. In a happy marriage it is your partner who backs you, serves as a confidant(e), trusted advisor and unselfish, reliable critic. Unfortunately not all marriages are that blessed and the strains of progressing in a career can be highly detrimental. Marriages are often threatened by one partner's unrelenting drive to succeed without considering the effects on the other. As in most situations in life, when opposing forces are threatening the equilibrium, wise compromises, tolerance and understanding may resolve conflicts, assure eventual success, perhaps slowing the vertiginous speed of one partner's career climb.

There are particular problems to be addressed in the two-career marriage, and this is the subject of the next section.

A prescription for a happy marriage of professionals includes:

> 1. Love to be together, even if it means skipping some business trips or research meetings that would enhance one's career.
> 2. Enjoy performing services for each other, even helping out with work assignments and studying extraneous material.
> 3. Treasure shared experiences, even those of working long hours that are needed to complete an assignment for one partner.
> 4. Trust each other, enjoy each other's successes and share any unhappiness over setbacks.

THE ROAD TO SUCCESS

> 5. Be available when the partner needs help even if it means altering one's own way of life and plans.
>
> 6. Give affection unstintingly, particularly when it is needed to lend support in crises.

These guidelines, easily enumerated but difficult to follow, will make a marriage partnership blossom. As stated, to achieve such harmony and actually enjoy doing favors for each other, requires discipline, strong will and more than just love; it demands total dedication to each other.

It takes maturity to realize that if one achieves the desired triumphs and they come at the expense of losing one's family bonds and remaining alone, it is an empty victory, exchanging lasting happiness for the fleeting pleasure of success.

Divorce is a depressing period in life for both partners. It causes unhappiness, threatens the stability of children and often destroys careers. This is ironical if the career climb and its demands were the root of the conflict.

The happy, lasting marriage is probably the most important background for enjoyment of life, for sailing safely through unavoidable difficulties, for being able to cope with life and career problems, small and large, and for looking back at one's life with warmth and satisfaction. But as in all partnerships, both members are responsible for its success or failure.

THE TWO-CAREER MARRIAGE

Both partners must be aware that they are members of one team and must support each other, even if sacrifices are required.

In our present society, where so much depends on a mutually acceptable living standard and on keeping up with the Joneses, financial solvency is essential to preserve a marriage. The lack of it is often a painfully sobering reality. The desired living standard in the United States and Western Europe is difficult to achieve today in most instances unless both partners have incomes. When these are pooled, the joint income will generally reach the desired level of spending. This level varies with aspirations, tastes, habits, and environment. It frequently clashes with what it is possible to achieve in real life considering the partners' earning capability.

The two-career marriage presents many possible complications that require careful handling, planning and often sacrifices from one or both partners. Many of the factors are pre-existing:

1. Educational background
2. Similarities or differences in professions or jobs
3. Equality or disparity in the level of position and income between the partners
4. Disparity in career achievement
5. Differences in age
6. Children
7. Location, location, location.

I will deal with each of these individually.

Educational background
Although this particular set of conditions is usually a present reality, it is frequently predetermined by where the partners meet at the start of the

relationship. When the relationship starts at work, there is generally a similarity in careers: lawyers, engineers, physicians, journalists etc. mingle with their colleagues in the place of employment. They bond by profession and sometimes the relationships have started in college.

When the educational background is different the best results happen when the partner with the higher educational achievement goes out of his or her way to help the other to advance their educational level, which will, over the long run, maintain equality in the relationship. If the partner who continues with education is a woman, this may delay having children. As educational level almost always affects status in business or in an educational institution, it is also reflected in income. Striving for equality is to be recommended. Both partners must be aware that they are members of one team; they should be supportive of each other. Career competition or envy of the other's success is destructive and should be consciously combated. This is more easily said than done. As it is uncommon for both partners to be equally successful, if a two-career marriage is to last it is essential for both partners to train themselves to enjoy their partner's success, as each will have undoubtedly contributed to the other. Each should realize that the success achieved by one partner also results in material, and many other, advantages for the whole family.

Similarities or differences in professions or jobs
It takes maturity to tolerate the high aspirations and excessive time investments of one's partner. Tastes, including interests and hobbies, are very likely to be much different if there is a difference in background and education. The length of hours on the job in order to succeed may be very different. And then there may be traveling. The greatest threat to any two-career marriage is the length of or repeated separations. The relocation of one partner due to transfer, career advancement or simply the only perceived chance of obtaining a good position for one of the partners can severely test the union.

The advice that can be given in such a set of circumstances is this:

> 1. Try to relocate together or do not let a separation last too long. Loneliness after work breeds new relationships and puts marriages in danger of breaking up.
> 2. Try to educate each other about your job. It may be fun and you will grow in mutual esteem.
> 3. Never deprecate your partner's occupation or profession.

THE TWO-CAREER MARRIAGE

Equality or disparity in education, background, or income of partners
It is only in fables or romantic movies that the prince marries Cinderella and they live happily ever after. This does not take into consideration the in-laws, the so-called friends, colleagues at work and neighbors. If the backgrounds, position and/or income are very disparate the partner with the disadvantage may decide to stay not to work, particularly if there are children, and act as a home partner trying to provide the best home atmosphere and support for the partner who is advancing in his or her career.

If, however, the disadvantaged partner feels too young and ambitious to accept this style of life, the answer may be to go back to school and work to change the disparity.

Disparity in career achievement
If both partners have not achieved equal status in their profession, maturity is required to enjoy a partner's success and not be jealous or envious. Consider yourself a partnership, in which each has responsibilities and provides support for the other. If income of both partners is needed to achieve the desired living standard, so that neither is able to become a home-partner, try to enjoy whatever career success you have. It may only be a question of time before conditions change, and one or both advance in career and income, leading to a satisfactory status.

Differences in age
Our society generally approves of a partnership in which the male partner is significantly older but frowns at the reverse. This is unfair but it is a reality (although it may be politically incorrect to state it). There is no reason for this distinction, but our lives and culture are filled with prejudices and inconsistencies. It takes love, courage, and faith on the part of both partners to triumph over society's fixed concepts. The prerequisites for a marriage with partners of very different age are:

> 1. Good physical, emotional and mental health enjoyed by both.
> 2. The younger partner accepts the unavoidable handicaps associated with age of the older partner.
> 3. Both partners must learn to tolerate the other's different tastes and habits associated with their generation.
> 4. There must be mutual respect.

With differences in age it is very likely that one partner may have been divorced or widowed. If there are children from previous marriages, it is essential that both partners treat them as their own, without favoritism. If handled correctly, the children will learn to regard both partners as their parents, even if they have visiting occasions with their other natural parent.

Children in a two-career marriage
As pointed out repeatedly above, a partner with a lesser position and income may find it fulfilling to stay with the children for at least their pre-school years. This will give the satisfaction of performing an enjoyable and valuable task. It is necessary that both partners value and respect this assignment.

The problems begin when both partners have career designs they deem to be important, and particularly when a bigger income is a priority. It is essential then to find compromises that will offer the children a safe, enticing, warm, and loving environment. It is important that children welcome the parents with joy when they come home. It is essential for one or preferably both parents to make every effort to have breakfast and dinner with the children and to be there when they go to sleep and to talk with them and make them feel loved. All this is possible if the income is sufficient to afford competent and responsible help.

Threatening problems may arise as the children reach adolescence. It is during the teenage years that particular attention must be paid to being with them as much as possible, to communicate and establish bonds and build confidence. Drugs and peer pressures can lead to tragedies. Both partners must do everything to solve children's problems even it means taking time off from a career. The message must be transmitted loudly that the parents care. Caring must be continued as children go to college, particularly if there were difficulties with studies or control of behavior. Make sure that prudent driving habits are learned and always observed.

The advice that parents should follow is not to choose a college for its prestige only. A university where you live or a junior college is preferable in order to be able to exercise needed supervision if there are any problems. If you cannot supervise whether your freshman is doing well in school, he or she may fail. Being away from home, on one's own, can be very threatening to a young, immature person, and studying and conforming may not be a priority. The temptations may be more than a very young person can cope with. Investing time and effort may be threatening to your career, but is very much worthwhile. If you don't do it, you will regret it forever.

Location
Where the two-career couple lives and works may be of tremendous importance in how they cope with life and its problems. Life is much simpler in

a small college town than in a metropolis. Advantages of small town living are:

> 1. Life is less expensive.
> 2. Coming home from work is much quicker as distances are shorter.
> 3. Social life and friendships are more structured and easier in a small town. This may further cement a marriage.
> 4. In smaller communities there is less anonymity, therefore self-control is exercised more easily and there are fewer temptations to go astray.
> 5. In a small town, outdoor activities, hikes, sight seeing, visiting places of historical significance are more common, bringing couples together.

Large cities offer other advantages:

> 1. Cultural activities are generally more abundant and of higher quality. There will be opportunities to go to the theater, concerts or even an opera. Going out together and enjoying the same events brings a couple closer together
> 2. If the couple's places of employment are not too far apart, commuting to work together is another way of communicating and planning life's activities.
> 3. There is a greater choice of good jobs, whether in a university or business.

Marriage is a fragile institution that needs constant work and, like plants, needs care and repeated addition of whatever is needed for growth and flowering. Your career should add quality to life and not be detrimental.

WORKING, ADVANCING IN A CAREER, AND ENJOYING LIFE

Out of your office, force yourself to stop thinking about the job and its problems. Have a social and cultural life, acquire hobbies, take vacations, and enjoy the only life you have.

Advancing one's career is stressful. The long hours, the continuous tension saps your energy and you feel that the pressures are only increasing, No matter how efficient you are, work never seems to be completed and you are always behind. Get used to it. It is not going to get better. You just will have to learn to cope.

You may not even have time to think between meetings or completing reports. In a university it will mean the continuous pressure of research grant applications. Preparing for all that may mean sleepless nights. You drive, or ride home, always late and, usually, making more calls on the cell phone. In the meantime your BlackBerry or Treo is giving you signals that there are more e-mail messages coming. You come home and if you have had a bad day at the office, you are preoccupied, short-tempered and basically not fun to be with, for either your partner or your children. Then after dinner, you will probably still ruminate about the bad day you have had, about the messages to answer and about preparing agendas, budgets, or experiments that are not succeeding. You go to bed, the last in the house, carefully trudging not to wake your sleeping family, and after tossing and turning you finally fall asleep. This may rarely be deep and refreshing, as you frequently have nightmares about what is facing you tomorrow and what you have not done.

Is there a way out? Psychologists or psychiatrists may be of little help as your behavior is within the normal range for a rising star in business or

THE ROAD TO SUCCESS

academia. Your reactions are those that most ambitious, active people in your position experience.

In order to make life and your successes enjoyable, you must learn that after you have left your office, you must stop thinking about the job and its problems. Have a social and cultural life, acquire hobbies, and take vacations.

The separation of job and private life is essential but not easily achieved. It takes discipline and a strong will to stop thinking about work and job-related problems. Try to listen to the news or your favorite music on the way home if you drive. If you are riding in a train or bus read an interesting novel or magazine. The length of the trip home helps you unwind. A single block walk is not sufficient. When you arrive home, try to start the evening with a glass of wine with your partner. Ask about what is new in

'This is nice hon. It almost makes me forget about the Henderson account.'

the household. If your partner also works inquire what is new in his or her life. Try not to talk about your job and issues related to it. There is so much happening in the world that one can talk about: politics, wars, theater, books, children, neighbors, plain gossip or future vacations. As the evening progresses the job-related problems fade, meld with those of the rest of the world and assume their proper significance. Falling asleep may be difficult, as the thoughts about work do not recede easily. One of the more successful ways to fall asleep is to keep repeating to yourself: 'Stop right now and fall asleep.' Block all other thoughts. It is unbelievably simple, and it works.

While this prescription works for some time, after a while the monotony takes its toll and alternate ways are needed to achieve peace of mind and avoid being a nuisance. Dining out with just your partner in an elegant restaurant creates its own magic. It feels as if the world has stopped and only you two are important. Weekend trips also help. Vacations to places that everyone in the family likes are a great way to rest, recuperate, and bond anew. When you take trips to conventions and to meetings of groups that you enjoy, take your partner with you if possible. If the meeting is being held abroad try to combine it with a vacation and some sight seeing.

Physical fitness is important. Try to exercise every day. For a busy person mornings before breakfast are the best time for exercise. In the evenings you are too tired, although some people prefer the evening hours in the gym. Physical exercise is a proven approach for unwinding. During the day you are probably too busy, but many companies encourage this way of spending the noon hour. Select a sport that you enjoy.

Do not limit yourself to one sport only. As you age, and all of us hopefully do, some sports become increasingly tiresome, and cause injuries, basketball for instance. Tennis is a wonderful sport for relaxing. It involves physical exercise, running and jumping, it is intellectually stimulating as you are trying to discover your opponent's weaknesses in order to play on them. You concentrate and forget everything else while playing. While young you play singles, and with doubles you can play well into old age and stay relatively fit. It is wise however to add another sport, which you can play when physical handicaps preclude the more demanding one. Golf is a good second sport, as you can gauge the amount of exercise, whether to walk or ride in a cart. Golf can be played for a long time as long as the legs and shoulders permit. If your partner also likes the same sport, do it together but do not compete against each other. After that, walking is still a possible way of staying fit. Joining a country club will help with finding suitable fitness facilities, tennis courts, and golf courses as well as making desirable social connections. Family

THE ROAD TO SUCCESS

memberships also help marriages and bringing up children. Join if you can possibly afford it; it does not need to be the most pretentious in town. Many universities' faculty clubs may have swimming pools, tennis courts and even golf courses. That may be another advantage of academic life!

'I still got it!'

PLANNING RETIREMENT

Retirement will surely come unless you die young. Avoid depending only on your pension. Always put away a certain amount of your income to save and invest before you pay your bills. Diversify your savings.

When you are young and full of ambition retirement planning is about the last thing you will think about. You are planning the next step in your career, the next material acquisition, and as your company or university has some type of health insurance for you and your family, even thinking of retirement is odious. It is associated with getting old, and that is not a flattering thought.

Yet most of us, except those who sadly die young due to accident or illness, do live to reach retirement age and it is important to plan for it. Find out about the pension plan of your company. With the industrial giants lately severely limiting or even canceling their pension plans (e.g. airlines, automobile manufacturing companies), with the prospective problems facing Social Security and Medicare, it is a good idea to have your own private disability insurance and retirement plan. This should be taken in addition to the one the company provides. Universities usually have more secure pension plans, although for state universities there is always the danger that in difficult budgetary times the governor may try to 'borrow' from the pension plan. It is now revealed that many companies were considering their pension funds to be their savings bank account from which to borrow without a chance of repayment.

It is therefore essential to make investments that will grow in order to make you financially independent when retirement arrives. Owning your home or apartment is a basic first step. Although real estate prices fluctuate, over time the slope is generally upward. The purchase of a home or apartment you can barely afford when you are young will become one of your best investments.

THE ROAD TO SUCCESS

Read about investments. There are many publications that are helpful as conditions change. Much information is also available on the Internet. Remember no expert is infallible and wise policy is to diversify: stocks, bonds, real estate, and possibly even consider a modest but informed investment in startup companies (only if you are thoroughly familiar with what they do). The odds of the latter are similar to betting on a horse and slightly better than winning the lottery.

Should you have financial advisors? If you can afford it, as they are expensive, select a good one, recommended by financially successful friends you trust. Realize however that investing is not a science; nobody can predict the future accurately.

The most important lesson about providing for old age, in addition to paying for the education of the children, helping them start out, financing unforeseen calamities, is to always put away a certain amount of your income before you pay your bills. It is crass but true: long-term financial stability is as important as good health, harmony of the family and a successful and enjoyable career.

Bibliography

FISHER, ROGER and URY, WILLIAM. *Getting to Yes: Negotiating Agreement without Giving In*, 10th edition. Penguin Books, New York, 1991
GARDNER, JOHN W. *On Leadership*. The Free Press, New York, 1990
GLADWELL, M. *The Tripping Point*. Little, Brown and Company, Boston, MA, 2000
GROVE, ANDREW S. *Only the Paranoid Survive*. Doubleday, New York, 1996
HAYWARD, STEVEN. *Churchill on Leadership – Executive Success in the Face of Adversity*. Forum (Prima Publishing), Rocklin, CA 1997
HEIM, PAT. *Hardball for Women*. Penguin Books, New York, 1993
HOWARD, PHILIP K. *The Death of Common Sense*. Warner Books, New York, 1996
HUNTSMAN, JON M. *Winners Never Cheat*. Wharton School Publishing, Upper Saddle River, NJ, 2005
JOHNSON, S. *Who Moved My Cheese?* G.P. Putnam's Sons, New York, 1998
KAYE, BEVERLY and JORDAN-EVANS, SHARON. *Love 'em or Lose 'em*. Berrett–Koehler, San Francisco, CA 1999
LENNICK, D. and KIEL, F. *Moral Intelligence*. Wharton School Publishing, Upper Saddle River, NJ, 2005
LOWE, JANET. *Jack Welch Speaks*. John Wiley & Sons, New York, 1998
MAXWELL, JOHN C. *The 21 Irrefutable Laws of Leadership*. Thomas Nelson Publishers, Nashville, 1988
MACHIAVELLI, NICCOLO. *The Prince [1515]*. Dover Thrift Series, Mineola, NY, 1992. Also available at http://www.constitution.org/mac/prince.txt
MORONE, JOSEPH G. *Winning in High Tech Markets*. Harvard Business School Press, Boston, MA, 1993
MUNDY, LINUS. *Slow-Down Therapy*. Abbey Press, St Meinard, IN, 1990
NATIONAL SCIENCE FOUNDATION GAO-04-639 Gender Issues: Women's Participation, 2004
PARKINSON, NORTHCOTE C. *Parkinson's Law*. Buccaneer Books, Cutchogue, NY, 1957
PETER, LAURENCE J. and HULL, RAYMOND. *The Peter Principle: Why Things Always Go Wrong*. William Morrow & Co., London, 1969
PETERS, T.J. and WATERMAN, R.H. Jr. *In Search of Excellence*. Warner Books, New York, 1982
PETERS, TOM. *Thriving on Chaos*. Video Publishing House, Schaumburg, IL, 1987
PHILLIPS, DONALD T. *Lincoln on Leadership*. Warner Books, New York, 1992

BIBLIOGRAPHY

SHEA, G.F. *Mentoring*, 3rd edition. Crisp Publications Inc, Menlo Park, CA, 2002

SUN-TZU, *The Art of Warfare* (translation by Roger Ames), Balantine Books, New York, 1993

WATERMAN, ROBERT H. JR. *The Renewal Factor*. Bantam Books, New York, 1987

WATT, FIONA M. Women in cell biology: getting to the top. *Nature Reviews Molecular Cell Biology* 7, 287–290 (April 2006); available at www.nature.com/nrm/archive/ index.html (accessed July 2006)

WATT, FIONA M. Women in cell biology: how personal lives shape careers. *Nature Reviews Molecular Cell Biology* 7, 378–380 (May 2006); available at www.nature.com/nrm/archive/index.html (accessed July 2006)

WECHSBERG, JOSEPH. *The Merchant Bankers*. Little Brown & Co., Boston, MA, 1966

WILSON, MIKE. *The Difference Between God and Larry Ellison*. William Morrow and Co., New York, 1997

WILSON PRICE, MARJORIE and MCLAUGHLIN, CURTIS P. *Leadership and Management in Academic Medicine*. Jossey-Bass Publishers, San Francisco, CA, 1984

ZACHARY, LOIS J. *The Mentor's Guide*. John Wiley and Sons Inc., San Francisco, CA, 2000

Index

Academia:
   advancing in, 23–30
   attributes, 4–5
   v. business, 23–30
   contributions, 23–4
   customs, 27
   extra-curricular income, 27
   failure, 26–7
   funding, 24, 28, 68
   gossip, 26
   idiosyncrasies, 26
   income, 27
   meetings, 24, 31–5
   mentoring, 76
   performance, 48
   pressures, 59–61
   promotion, 24–5, 29–30
   space, 24
   tenure, 28–9, 63–4
Accomplishment records, 4, 23
Advancement, career, 23–30, 93–6
Advisory positions *v.* executive positions, 10
Age differences, two-career marriages, 89-90
Aides:
   loyalty, 51–52
   respect, 51–52
   time management, 54
Allies, meetings, 33
Ambition, 1, 3
   mismatch, 4
   peers, 59
   testing, 3–4
Approachability/familiarity, 51
Assistants, entertaining, 83–4
Athena Project, women, 20
Attire *see* Dress
Attitudes, 3
   gender differences, 16–17, 50
   gender discrimination, 15

Attributes:
   academia, 4–5
   business, 5
   negative, 5–7
   positive, 4–5
   professional success, 4–5
   promotion, 4–5

Background issues, two-career marriages, 89
Barriers to CEOs, 27
Benefits, promotion, 30
BlackBerrys, 44–6
Board meetings, 31–5
Brain differences, gender, 15–16
Business:
   v. academia, 23–30
   advancing in, 23–30
   attributes, 4–5
   customs, 27
   failure, 26–7
   funding, 25, 70
   gossip, 26
   idiosyncrasies, 27
   meetings, 31–5
   mentoring, 76–7
   performance, 50
   pressures, 59–61
   promotion, 25–7, 29–30
   space, 25
   tenure, 28–9

Career achievement, two-career marriages, 89
Career advancement, 23–30, 93–6
   Faustian bargain, 9–11
   stress, 9–11, 93
Career entry trends, postgraduate degrees, 71-2
Career/family issues *see* Family/career issues
Cerberus, 27

101

INDEX

Chairing meetings, 34, 54
Chance, 1, 14
Chastising, 51
Chiefs:
   see also Superiors
   as allies, 57–65
   consistency, 13–14
   cooperation, 13
   evaluating, 62–4
   hostile, 61-5
   images, 13–14
   new, 58–65
   planning, 13
   popularity, 14
   predictability, 13–14
   presentations, 60–61
   pressures, 59-61
   proximity, 60
   types, 13–14
   women, 64–5
Children, two-career marriages, 89–90
Clear thinking, 64
Colleagues:
   loyalty, 50–51
   respect, 50-51
Committee meetings, 31–5
Compromise, women, 19
Computers, gender differences, 16
Confrontations, 23
Consensus, meetings, 31
Consistency, chiefs, 13–14
Contributions, academia, 24–5
Conversation, entertaining, 82–3
Cooperation, chiefs, 13
Courage, 3, 64
Cultural life, 93–6
Culture:
   meetings, 32–3
   presentations, 33-4
Customs, 27

Degrees:
   educational, 4
   MBAs, 71–3
   PhDs, 71–3
   postgraduate, 71–3
Demeanor under stress, 3
Disappointments, 7
Discrimination, gender, 15
Dog fable, 64
Dog teams, 50
Dress:
   see also Physical appearance

   entertaining, 81
   importance, 37–8
   interviews, 69
   meetings, 35
   presentations, 33
   women, 35
Drinking, entertaining, 80-81, 82, 83

E-mail, 45–6
Educational background, two-career
     marriages, 87–8, 89
Educational degrees, 4
Efficiency, 5
   time management, 53–5
Engineering positions, gender differences, 17
Enjoying life, 93–6
Entertaining, 79–84
   assistants, 83–4
   basic rule, 79
   conversation, 82–3
   dress, 81
   drinking, 80–81, 82, 83
   equals, 83
   gender differences, 84
   at home, 82
   peers, 83
   at restaurants, 79–81
   seating, 81
   superiors, 79–83
Entertaining presentations, 33
Equals, entertaining, 83
Equipment, offices, 42–4
Errors of judgement, avoiding, 5–7
Ethical behavior, 1
Ethical rules, 4
Evaluating:
   chiefs, 62–4
   meetings, 31–2
   new jobs, 68-9
Executive positions, *v.* advisory
     positions, 10
Exercise, physical, 95–6
Expenses, reducing, 5
Exploitation, women, 21
External circumstances, 3
Extra-curricular income, academia, 27

Failure:
   academia, 26–7
   business, 26–7
Familiarity/approachability, 51
Family/career issues:
   see also Two-career marriages

INDEX

marriage issues, 85–6
postgraduate degrees, 73
women, 18–19
Fast track postgraduate degrees, 73
Faustian bargain, career advancement, 9–11
Financial stability, 97–8
Finding new jobs, 61–2, 63, 67–70
First jobs, 67
   see also New jobs
Functionality, time management, 55
Funding:
   academia, 24, 27, 70
   business, 25, 70
   extra-curricular income, 27
   income issues, two-career marriages, 89
   new jobs, 70
Furniture, offices, 43–4

Game plan, time management, 53
Gender differences, 15–21
   see also Women
   attitudes, 16–17, 50
   brain differences, 15–16
   computers, 16
   engineering positions, 17
   entertaining, 84
   gender discrimination, 15
   glass ceiling, 15, 17–18
   law, 18
   medicine, 17
   promotion, 50
   science positions, 17
   social issues, 50
Gifts, innate, 3–8
Glass ceiling, 15, 17–18
'Golden parachutes', 28, 63
Gossip, 26, 47, 63

Harassment:
   offices, 44
   sexual, 21
Home, entertaining at, 82
Hostile chiefs, 61–5

Idiosyncrasies, 27
Image:
   chiefs, 13–14
   offices, 41–2
Income, academia, 27
Income issues, two-career marriages, 89
Innate gifts, 3–8
Integrity, 1
Intelligence, 3

Interviews:
   answers, 69
   dress, 69
   negotiating, 69
   new jobs, 69
   preparation, 69
   rules, 69
Investigating new jobs, 68, 70
Investments, 97–8

Job similarities/differences, two-career marriages, 88
Jobs, new *see* New jobs

Lateral arabesques, 10, 23–4, 29
Law:
   gender differences, 18
   litigation, 61, 63
Line jobs, *v.* staff jobs, 10
Locations:
   meetings, 54
   two-career marriages, 90–91
Logical solution, promotion, 7–8
Loyalty, 49–52
   aides, 51–2
   colleagues, 50–51
   staff, 51–52
   superiors, 49–50
Luck, 1, 14
Lunches, superiors, 82–3

Marriage issues, 85–6, 91
   see also Family/career issues; Two-career marriages
Mathematical approach, promotion, 7–8
MBAs, 70–73
Medicine, gender differences, 17
Meetings, 31–5
   academia, 24, 31–5
   allies, 32
   board, 31–5
   business, 31–5
   chairing, 34, 54
   committee, 31–5
   consensus, 31
   culture, 32–3
   dress, 35
   evaluating, 31–2
   locations, 54
   PowerPoint presentations, 32–3
   preparation, 59
   presentations, 32–4
   speaking at, 33, 34

103

INDEX

Meetings (*Contd*)
   subjects, 31–2
   time management, 54
   timing, 33
   women, 34–5
Mentoring, 3–5, 24, 75–8
   academia, 76
   business, 76–7
   choosing a mentor, 75–8
   large companies, 77
   purpose, 75
   small companies, 77
   types, 76
   women, 20–1, 77–8
Mistakes, promotion, 29–30

Negative attributes, 5–7
Negotiating, interviews, 69
Negotiating successfully, new jobs, 67–70
Nepotism, 51
Networking, women, 20–21
New jobs:
   evaluating, 68–9
   finding, 61–2, 63
   first jobs, 67
   funding, 70
   interviews, 69
   investigating, 68, 70
   negotiating successfully, 67–70
   promotion, 68, 70
   reason for vacancy, 70
   space, 70

Obesity, 39
Offices, 41–4
   equipment, 42–4
   furniture, 43–4
   harassment, 44
   image, 41–2
   pecking order, 42
   views, 42
Opposing presentations, 34

Paranoia, 29
Pasteur's maxim, 1, 14
Pecking order, offices, 42
Peers:
   ambition, 59
   entertaining, 83
Pensions, 97–8
Performance, 50
Personal qualities, general, 5
Peter's Principles, 10

PhDs, 71-3
Physical appearance, 3, 6, 39–40
   see also Dress
Physical exercise, 95–6
Planning:
   chiefs, 13
   retirement, 97–8
Poodle fable, 64
Popularity, chiefs, 14
Positive assets:
   professional success, 4–5
   promotion, 4–5
Positive attributes, 4–5
Postgraduate degrees, 71-3
   career entry trends, 71–2
   family/career issues, 73
   fast track, 73
PowerPoint presentations, meetings, 32–3
Praise, 51
Predictability, chiefs, 13–14
Preparation:
   interviews, 69
   meetings, 59
Presentations:
   chiefs, 60–61
   good, 33–4
   meetings, 32–4
   opposing, 34
   PowerPoint, 33
   rehearsing, 33
Pressures:
   see also Stress
   dealing with, 59–61
Pride in belonging, 52
Private life, 93–6
   see also Marriage issues
Productivity, increasing, 5
Professional success:
   attributes, 4–5
   positive assets, 4–5
Promotion:
   academia, 24–5, 29–30
   attributes, 4–5
   benefits, 30
   business, 25–7, 29–30
   gender differences, 50
   glass ceiling, 15, 17–18
   logical solution, 7–8
   mathematical approach, 7–8
   mistakes, 29–30
   new jobs, 68, 70
   paths, 29–30
   policies, 18

positive assets, 4–5
reactions to, 50
relative importance, 11
women, 11
working for, 51

Recommendations, making, 59
Records of accomplishment, 4, 23
Rehearsing presentations, 33
Resigning, 61-2, 63, 65
Respect, 49–52
   aides, 51–2
   colleagues, 50–51
   staff, 51–52
   superiors, 49–50
Restaurants, entertaining at, 79–81
Retirement, planning, 97–8
Role models, 51
Roman custom, 13
Rules of life, 1

Sacrificing, 3, 9–11
Savings, 97–8
Science positions, gender differences, 17
Seating, entertaining, 81
Self-respect, 1
Sexual harassment, women, 21
Sleep, 95
Social issues, gender differences, 50
Social life, 93–6
Space:
   academia, 24
   business, 25
   new jobs, 70
Speaking at meetings, 33, 34
Sport, 95–6
Staff:
   loyalty, 51-3
   respect, 51-2
   time management, 54
Staff jobs *v.* line jobs, 10
Stress:
   career advancement, 9–11, 93
   demeanor under, 3
Success:
   new jobs, 67–70
   professional, 4–5
Superiors:
   see also Chiefs
   as allies, 57–65

entertaining, 79–83
loyalty, 49–50
lunches, 82–3
respect, 49–50

Telephoning, 44, 48
   time management, 53
Tenure:
   academia, 28–9, 63–4
   business, 28–9
Thinking clearly, 64
Time management, 53–5
   aides, 54
   budgeting time, 53–5
   efficiency, 53–5
   functionality, 55
   game plan, 53
   meetings, 54
   presentations, 33
   staff, 54
   telephoning, 53
Treachery, 64
Treos, 44–6
Two-career marriages, 87–91
   age differences, 89–90
   background issues, 89
   career achievement, 89
   children, 89–90
   educational background, 87–8, 89
   income issues, 89
   job similarities/differences, 88
   locations, 90–91
Tyrants, 23–4

Why me?, 7
Women, 15–21
   see also Gender differences
   Athena Project, 20
   compromise, 19
   dress, 35
   exploitation, 21
   family/career issues, 18–19
   hostile chiefs, 64–5
   meetings, 34–5
   mentoring, 20–1, 77–8
   networking, 20–1
   promotion, 11, 15, 17–18
   sexual harassment, 21